Alternative Facts

CAN YOU TELL WHICH STORIES ARE REAL?

200
Incredible,
Absolutely
True(-ish)
Stories

....

Alex Palmer

FALL RIVER PRESS

New York

FALL RIVER PRESS

New York

An Imprint of Sterling Publishing Co., Inc.
1166 Avenue of the Americas
New York, NY 10036

ISBN 978-1-4351-6627-1

Distributed in Canada by Sterling Publishing Co., Inc.
c/o Canadian Manda Group, 664 Annette Street
Toronto, Ontario, Canada M6S 2C8
Distributed in the United Kingdom by GMC Distribution Services
Castle Place, 166 High Street, Lewes, East Sussex, England BN7 1XU
Distributed in Australia by NewSouth Books
45 Beach Street, Coogee, NSW 2034, Australia

For information about custom editions, special sales, and premium and corporate
purchases, please contact Sterling Special Sales at 800-805-5489 or
specialsales@sterlingpublishing.com.

Manufactured in the United States of America

2 4 6 8 10 9 7 5 3 1

sterlingpublishing.com

Cover design by Igor Stravinsky
Interior design by Sharon Jacobs

Table of Contents

Introduction v

CHAPTER 1
Skinny Jeans, Vaseline, and Frisbee 1

CHAPTER 2
Dracula, Bubonic Plague, and
Knock-Knock Jokes 43

CHAPTER 3
Jet Lag, Jellyfish, and Cricket Ears 85

CHAPTER 4
Outhouses, Oreos, and Niagara Falls 125

CHAPTER 5
High Heels, Hokey Pokey, and
Piggy Banks 167

ALTERNATIVE FACTS SCORE CARD AND ANSWER SHEET 208

ANSWER KEY 219

INTRODUCTION

*S***top me if** this sounds familiar: you are scrolling through the news or social media posts on your phone when you come across a story that's too crazy to be true. It might be an unbelievable fact about some everyday thing, a hilarious story about someone doing something idiotic, or another example of bad behavior from a politician who makes your blood boil. You share the story or send it to friends, asking, "Can you believe this?" only to have one of them write back, "That's not actually true."

It's a bit embarrassing. But we've all been there. We are bombarded by anecdotes, opinions, news, and fake news at a rate unimaginable just a generation ago. Figuring out what is true and what is false (and more likely, what is in the gray area in-between) isn't always easy, particularly when we're eager to share an amazing story with our friends.

Of course, we have always had to untangle what's true from what's too-good-to-be-true. Before fake news and alternative facts, we had urban legends, tall tales, and ancient myths. But these fabrications used to float from person to person, and generation to generation, at a glacial pace. Now they come at us from ten directions at once, and at the speed of light— or at least a high-speed Internet connection. To function in today's information-intensive environment, we must be lightning-fast traffic conductors, sending the truth in one direction and falsehood in the other, with only our instincts (and the occasional Google search) as our guide.

That is where *Alternative Facts* comes in. Think of this book as a game to help you cultivate your fact-finding senses—to help you develop an ear for stories that do not ring true, an eye for fake news, and a nose that can sniff out BS. Or just think of it as an entertaining bathroom read—that can at times be full of you-know-what.

*H*ere's how this book works: it contains exactly two hundred entries, organized into five fairly random sections, including weird bits about the human body, unexpected anecdotes about famous figures, morsels about strange animal behavior, and scary findings about our favorite foods and drinks. Most of them are true and will hopefully surprise you, even making you rethink assumptions you held about some of the most familiar things in your daily life. But about one-third of them are Alternative Facts. These are tidbits that are interesting and seem like they could be true. They are tempting to believe and in some cases you may have believed them yourself for years. But they are bunk.

After you read an entry, decide whether it was a **Fact** or an **Alternative Fact**, then flip to its corresponding number in the back of the book to see which it was. For Facts, you'll find a source to verify the truth of the entry. For the Alternative Facts, there is an explanation for why it's false—in some cases the whole thing is made up; in others it takes a partial truth and warps it into something ridiculous. For those who like to keep score or who want to compete with friends, we've included an answer sheet at the back of the book where you can jot your predictions as you read. Then check which were true or false at the end and use the scorecard to rate your fact-finding skills.

So let's get on with it—on to *Alternative Facts!*

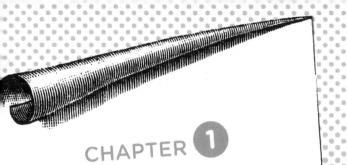

CHAPTER 1

Skinny Jeans, Vaseline, and Frisbee

"**The truth** does not change according to our ability to stomach it."

—*Flannery O'Connor*

1

Sitting too close to the television set is not actually bad for your eyes. This was true more than fifty years ago, when General Electric's new color televisions emitted levels of radiation considered by federal health officials as far too high to be safe. But after GE recalled these sets, there have been effectively no cases of televisions causing physical damage to TV watchers or their eyes, no matter how close they sit. For those with a wall-sized flat-screen TV, there is probably no need to sit a few inches from the screen, anyway—or even be in the same room.

2

S kinny jeans can be bad for your health. The fashionable attire has been linked to *meraligia parasthetica*. Also known as "tingling thigh syndrome," the condition occurs when pressure cuts off the lateral femoral cutaneous nerve, leading to symptoms that include numbness and sunburn-like pain. Toward the end of the first decade of the 2000s, doctors reported an uptick in the ailment in young people and attributed it to the popularity of skin-tight denim. Another factor that caused a tilting of the pelvis and compressed the nerve further was found to increase the likelihood of developing tingling thigh syndrome: wearing high heels.

3

Toilet paper took a long time to catch on. Prior to the "rollout" of a more convenient bathroom tissue, Americans were in the habit of using old newspapers and catalogs to take care of business. When inventor Joseph Gayetty rolled out bathroom tissue, it came in packs of flat, individual sheets that struck most consumers as a waste (why buy brand-new papers for such a distasteful purpose?) and it sold poorly. It would be a British businessman who would come upon the idea of putting the paper into perforated rolls—and a pair of New Yorkers who knew how to market it—who finally popularized the product in the 1880s. Old newspapers everywhere rejoiced.

4

Before rubber became a popular material for erasers, people used bread crumbs. The soft bits of baked flour and water, shaped into small balls, were surprisingly effective at removing the marks of pencils and charcoal. English engineer Edward Nairne realized in 1770 that rubber could get the job done, but the use of rubber in erasers did not really take off until Charles Goodyear's vulcanization process created more durable and effective eraser material in 1839, and soon it was being added to the bottom of pencils (something that probably would not have worked too well with bread crumbs). But as late as 1891, art magazines were still instructing those creating charcoal illustrations, "If lights are lost, they may be restored by using soft, stale bread crumbs, rolled between the fingers and shaped into either a flat or pointed lump as necessity requires."

5

𝒱*aseline was* originally marketed as an edible health supplement. Promising a wide range of benefits, from aiding digestion to quelling heartburn, the manufacturers urged Americans to eat "a spoonful at every meal" to enjoy the petroleum extract's full advantages. It failed to catch on when first released in the 1870s, partly due to the jelly's off-putting flavor and texture. When it was rebranded as a *topical* healing agent that soothed cuts, burns, and chapped lips, the material took off. Nonetheless, Vaseline's inventor, Robert Chesebrough, continued to eat a spoonful of the stuff every day—and lived to the ripe age of ninety-six.

6

Q-tips used to be called Baby Gays. Leo Gerstenzang, founder of the Leo Gerstenzang Infant Novelty Co., which marketed baby care accessories, came upon the idea of cotton swabs while watching his wife creating makeshift ones with cotton balls and toothpicks. He marketed them to parents, dubbing the swabs Q-tips Baby Gays (the "Q" stood for quality, the "tips" for the tips of the swabs, and, we can only guess, "Gays" for how happy they would make babies when used to clean their ears, nostrils, and eyes). Unlike today, the cotton was wrapped around a wooden stick, constructed by hand, and dipped in boric acid to aid in cleaning. The product caught on but the wood became plastic, machines took over the manufacturing, and both the boric acid and "Baby Gays" in the name were eighty-sixed.

7

𝒯he expression "to eighty-six" —as in, to get rid of something or eject someone—came from the fact that eighty-six was the New York City police code for the illegal sale of alcohol. Throughout Prohibition, speakeasy operators would pay off the New York Police Department in order to keep their doors open. Those who failed to pay their regular bribe to the boys in blue would be told to pay up "or else we will eighty-six you," i.e., actually enforce the law against selling alcohol. The threats worked, keeping the illicit economy thriving and the pockets of the local policemen lined with cash. Even after Prohibition was repealed, the expression stuck, though now it is more likely to refer to the removal of a drunken patron from a bar rather than the closure of the bar itself.

8

Before the invention of pockets, men stored things in their codpieces. The accessory began as a simple triangle of cloth to cover the gap between a man's doublet and hose. But it became increasingly elaborate and decorative over time, reaching its jeweled apex during the reign of Henry VIII. Constructed with a fastened flap and stuffed with cloth, it served as a roomy place to store money, personal effects, or even a small weapon (in Middle English, the word *cod* actually meant "bag" as well as "scrotum"). Eventually the style fell out of fashion, replaced by a small cloth drawstring bag hung from a man's waist, then inserted into a seam in his pants, then finally sewn permanently into the garment.

9

Anne Boleyn had eleven fingers. King Henry VIII's second wife and key figure in the start of the English Reformation had "on her right hand, six fingers" according to a contemporary account. Such polydactylism (the formal name of having extra fingers or toes) was not unusual in the era before developments in medicine made the removal of unwanted digits a simple surgery. The extra finger was likely not a fully functioning one, and it was formed from soft tissue around a small bone without joints. By all accounts, she wore her wedding ring, while she had one, on the same ring finger as anyone else.

Boleyn's daughter, Queen Elizabeth I, may be the epitome of royal elegance in her portraits, but she could cuss with the best of them. According to the *Dictionary of National Biography*, the Virgin Queen "swore, she spat upon a courtier's coat when it did not please her taste, she beat her gentlewomen soundly, she kissed whom she pleased." Another historian described how during a courtship from French Duke Francis of Anjou and Alençon she "broke into strong language, as was her wont, and … [swore] like a trooper."

11

While Elizabeth I was reputed to think little of her late mother, rarely mentioning her, in fact there is plenty of evidence she had very fond feelings for her. In her teenage years, she wore Boleyn's famous "A" pendant when posing for a portrait (and likely on more occasions than that). As queen, she worked to place her ill-fated mother's relatives in prominent positions on the court and took to wearing a different pendant that held a miniature portrait of her opposite a portrait of her mother—hardly the actions of an ungrateful daughter.

12

The word silhouette comes from a notoriously frugal French minister, Étienne de Silhouette, who served as France's Comptroller General in 1759, a time of economic difficulty. He had the unpleasant assignment of curbing his country's spending to keep its deficit from spiraling further out of control. He did so by levying taxes not just on the wealthy but on anything that signaled wealth—luxury goods, decorative furnishings, servants, and more. Anything elaborate was out, and anything bare-bones was in (and was referred to as à la Silhouette). No wonder, under this kind of pressure, that opulent paintings fell out of fashion at the time, as simple black-and-white outlines of individuals grew in popularity—and came to be named after the man most associated with the era's miserly ways.

13

Worse than being a notorious miser might be the fate of John Duns Scotus. The Scottish philosopher-humanitarian of the Middle Ages was given the papal title "the Subtle Doctor" and contributed many influential ideas to questions about the nature of human freedom and "divine illumination." But his legacy for the average non-philosopher is the word *dunce*. His followers, known as "Dunsmen," maintained their mentor's highly complicated logic about the nature of humanity even as it fell out of fashion, leading them to be ridiculed by the more forward-thinking folks of the Renaissance. The Dunsmen also had a habit of wearing pointy hats—a custom practiced by Scotus himself. The perceived ignorance and backward learning of these men led *dunce* to become associated with a person slow at learning, and the dunce cap to be a mark of ignorance and shame.

14

The word blooper *originated in the military. It was the nickname given to a bolt-action rifle used by Americans in World War I. Formally known as the Browning–Lester rifle, it became shortened to BL rifle, then just "the blooper." It quickly proved unpopular when it jammed during rifle training exercises and soldiers protested being sent into war with weapons of questionable reliability. The U.S. Army agreed that the firearms were less than dependable. The bloopers never saw active battle, and they ceased to be manufactured soon after. Although the rifles were never heard of again, the term* blooper *as a euphemism for "mistake," particularly in the heat of competition, stuck.*

15

*B*aseball *was* invented by a Civil War soldier named Abner Doubleday. A moderately successful combat general, he earned much greater fame as the man who came up with America's favorite pastime, sketching out the first baseball diamond in a pasture in Cooperstown, New York, in 1839. His contribution wasn't known until 1905, when the National League set out to trace the origins of the game and uncovered the story of Doubleday. The National Baseball Hall of Fame is housed in Doubleday's hometown and his name adorns Doubleday Field, the pasture where the game began.

16

PLAYER
OF THE DAY

Before he led the Cuban revolution and eventually became the country's president, Fidel Castro tried out for the New York Yankees. He was a passionate fan of baseball and a very skilled player, so when the Yankees went scouting for new members in Havana, Castro was a prime prospect. Little information remains about how he performed in his tryout, but presumably it did not go great—if it had, perhaps the Cuban Revolution would have played out very differently.

17

*T*he *Pittsburgh* Steelers and Philadelphia Eagles combined to form the Steagles for their 1943 season. With so many players fighting in World War II, the Steelers were down to just six men and the Eagles just over twice that, with many of those drafted in the 1943 NFL Draft also going off to fight. The NFL commissioner suggested merging the two, and the team owners came around to the idea, even if the players still saw each other as rivals and the head coaches (who became cohead coaches) hated each other's guts. After a few initial stumbles, the merged team (formally known as "Phil-Pitt") went on to a 5–4–1 record—the first winning season in the Eagles' history, and the second for the Steelers.

18

Golf is actually an acronym for "Gentlemen Only, Ladies Forbidden." The term was first used in Scotland in reference to a game in which players used measured and smoothed-down sticks to strike balls —slightly larger than modern golf balls—into holes. At the time there were concerns that all those sticks flying could cause injury to the "delicate wives and daughters," as one Scot wrote in a letter describing the game (or perhaps they just wanted some guy time). Whatever the reasons, as the game evolved and cooled it with the sexism, the name stuck.

20

Cabbage Patch Kids originated as an artist's concept of how children would appear if exposed to nuclear radiation in the womb. As the Reagan administration prepared for possible thermonuclear war during the 1980s, it reached out to scientists, researchers, and artists to help it understand radiation's effects, as part of a public awareness and emergency preparedness campaign. Artist Xavier Roberts designed the dolls to help with this public education, but the initiative never got past the concept stage. When the government made clear that it would no longer need Roberts' services, the artist sold his design to toymaker Coleco in 1983 and the "mutant babies" became a massive hit.

21

Frisbees are named after a pie. The Frisbie Pie Company (founded by a fellow named William Russell Frisbie) sold baked goods from its Bridgeport, Connecticut, headquarters starting in the 1870s. But it wasn't until the 1950s when a toy manufacturer, conducting campus tours as he sought to popularize a UFO-like flying saucer toy, noted the popularity of tossing pie tins on New England university campuses, which students called "Frisbie-ing." It caught on across the world, making him a fortune, not a dime of which went to Bill Frisbie's heirs.

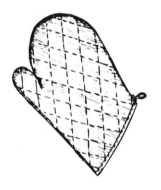

*B*etty Crocker was a real person. The wife of William Crocker, an executive at the Washburn-Crosby Company (which would later merge to become part of General Mills), Betty frequently hosted dinner parties for the company's leaders and dazzled them with her cooking. When seeking a way to personalize the company's new food and recipe brand in the 1920s, a member of the team suggested Betty's name, initially in jest, but the moniker stuck.

23

Famous Amos was also a real person. A talent agent for the William Morris Agency (where he worked with the Supremes, Simon & Garfunkel, and Marvin Gaye), Wally Amos would send packages of homemade cookies to friends and prospective clients. He got such a great response from his baked goods that, in the 1970s, he borrowed $25,000 and launched Famous Amos. It proved a smart gamble, bringing in more than $1 million in sales during its second year of operation. Though Amos sold the company in 1988, he never stopped baking, launching The Cookie Kahuna cookie business in 2014.

24

The Michelin Man is actually named Bibendum. Édouard and André Michelin, the tire company's founders, conceived the idea in 1894 at the Exposition Universelle in Lyon, France, when they saw a stack of tires and realized it looked like an armless man—and a perfect mascot for their company. They tapped cartoonist Marius Rossillon to sketch out the character that the founders had in mind. He had just the thing: a large, jolly figure, hoisting a beer glass, which he had originally drawn for a Munich brewery. Rossillon made a few tweaks to the image, removing the beer and making the man appear to be constructed of tires. But they liked Rossilon's tagline—a phrase from Horace's *Odes* that read *Nunc est bibendum* ("Drink up"). The Michelin brothers took the last word and made it the character's name, Bibendum ("Bib" to his friends, and "Michelin Man" to everyone else in the world).

25

Charlie Brown, Lucy, Linus, and the rest of the gang were called "Radishes," rather than "Peanuts," in Denmark (and "Little Radishes" in South America). The *Peanuts* comic strips were internationally popular, appearing in more than twenty-six thousand newspapers across seventy-five countries, but because the word didn't have the same diminutive meaning in Danish and Spanish as it had in English, the strip was renamed to the more locally familiar *Radishes*.

26

Donkey Kong's name was the result of a mistranslation. Nintendo designer and video game pioneer Shigeru Miyamoto was charged with creating a game in which the hero attempts to save a damsel in distress from a King Kong–like villain. Due to copyright concerns, the company could not give the character the same name as the famed movie monster, so they opted for a more literal choice: Monkey Kong (the title the game still holds in Japan). But when sending instructions to the American importers for the game design, a typo on the fax led to the character erroneously becoming "Donkey Kong" and the name stuck.

27

Cat lovers, skip this one: one of the weirdest instruments ever invented was the *katzenklavier* —also known as the cat organ. This piano, devised by seventeenth-century German Jesuit inventor Athanasius Kircher, placed seven to nine felines— each corresponding to a different pitch—in cages, with their tails outstretched and secured in place. A nail would be pressed onto each tail to elicit a hiss or shriek from the animal at the right moment to create a "song." Fortunately for all involved, while Kircher drew up detailed plans, the instrument never got past the idea stage.

28

NERO.

$\mathcal{T}$*he expression* "Nero fiddled while Rome burned" is wrong on a few counts. In July of 64 AD, when about 70 percent of the city was destroyed in a massive six-day fire, Emperor Nero was out of town—at his villa in Antium, some thirty-five miles outside of Rome. Also, even if he had been in Rome, he probably would not have been fiddling. The *viol* class of instruments, of which the fiddle is a member, was not developed until the eleventh century.

29

The loudest musical instrument ever invented is likely the *Gjallarhorn*. The massive horn with a twisting crook that wrapped around the player was used by Vikings in burial ceremonies. Musicologists estimate it would have been able to reach a volume of 140 decibels when it was originally used. Unfortunately, only one has been found fully intact and they have been unable to actually test it, out of concern that playing it might damage the ancient instrument.

30

S ince 2000, Finland has played host to the Mobile Phone Throwing World Championships. Each competitor is given an "official phone," which he or she throws over his or her shoulder —the person who throws it the farthest wins. There's also a "freestyle" category in which teams of up to three people are judged based on their "style and aesthetics" and "overall appearance." In 2013, Riku Haverinen, a native Finn, took home the prize by chucking his phone 320.64 feet (97.7m). While originated in Finland, other phone-throwing competitions have since popped up in Switzerland, the Czech Republic, the United States, and elsewhere. Turns out people everywhere are eager to express anger at their phones.

31

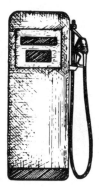

Using a cell phone while pumping gas will not spark an explosion. Thanks to rumors, false news reports, and even signs posted at gas stations and warnings included in wireless phone manuals, the belief that using a mobile phone near a gas pump could ignite flammable materials has caught on like wildfire. The Federal Communications Commission dug into this and found no link between wireless phones and fuel vapors. As the FCC puts it, "there is no documented incident where the use of a wireless phone was found to cause a fire or explosion at a gas station."

32

Speaking of gas stations, next time you need to fuel up, make sure you do it in the morning or later at night. When temperatures are cooler, gasoline is denser, and you get more fuel per gallon pumped into your tank. One study compared the fuel usage of gas pumped when outside temperatures are 40°F (4.4°C) compared to 90°F (32.2°C). Cars filled with gas in the colder temperature ran an average of 4 percent longer than cars pumped when it was warmer. Multiply that by several tanks and the savings might make it worth getting up a little earlier in the morning.

33

*M*odel *T* Fords came in many colors besides black: brown, maroon, green, and light blue, to name a few. The conventional belief that the model was available only in black is rooted in the fact that, for a few years during and after the First World War, the classic black became the only option, likely because it was the most efficient and durable available choice (and according to some accounts, dried faster than other colors). This was when Ford famously said, "You can have any color as long as it's black". But at the time it was first introduced and later in the 1920s, the Ford came in many shades.

34

When called home in 1945, hundreds of American soldiers stationed in southern Belgium realized that they wouldn't be able to bring the cars they had been driving back with them. So they simply abandoned their vehicles, intending to come back for them at some point in the future. They hid the cars in the forested region of Châtillon, lining them up in an area that was unlikely to see many passersby. More than seven decades later, a few of the soldiers returned to the "car graveyard" to find the cars rotted and scavenged for pieces. The rusting carcasses (pun intended) of more than five hundred automobiles covered by a resurgent forest looked like something out of a post-apocalyptic zombie movie. But any soldiers still hoping to get their cars will be sorely disappointed: the Belgian government finally cleared most of the metal skeletons in 2010.

35

The Germans occupied a part of the United Kingdom during the Second World War. In the summer of 1940, Hitler's forces invaded the demilitarized Channel Islands, an archipelago under British rule, set off the French coast near Normandy, in the English Channel. They set up an administration on the islands of Jersey and Guernsey, enforcing German military law, confiscating radios, deporting citizens, and even changing the time zone to Germany's local time. Some islanders resisted, publishing underground newspapers or sheltering escaped slave workers, and others attempted to escape. But Britain made few attempts to regain control of the islands, and it remained under German authority until the war ended in 1945.

36

The role of Rick in *Casablanca*, famously played by Humphrey Bogart, was originally played by Ronald Reagan. The two were both rising stars at the time and the film's producers had worked with Reagan in two previous films, which gave him the edge in the casting of the film. But after filming a few scenes with him in the lead, the United States entered the war and the future president decided to enlist in the Cavalry Reserve, and he was forced to back out of what ended up being the role of a lifetime. Fortunately he had other prospects in his future.

37

Before it was an "Oscar," the Academy Award was briefly known as a "Tracy." Actor Spencer Tracy won back-to-back Best Actor awards in 1938 for *Captains Courageous* and 1939 for *Boys Town* (on top of being nominated in 1937 for *San Francisco*). At a time before the little gold men had a first name, Tracy became the default moniker. Members of the industry began informally referring to the awards as "the Tracys" and the industry trades followed suit. In the 1940 show, no fewer than three presenters referred to them as "the Tracys." But in the end, Oscar was the name that stuck.

38

*O*scar winners used to be announced before the ceremony. For most of the 1930s, the Academy gave newspapers the names in advance, with the agreement that they would not publish the names until 11 p.m. The *Los Angeles Times* broke this rule during the heated 1940 competition (which included *Stagecoach, Gone with the Wind, Mr. Smith Goes to Washington,* and *The Wizard of Oz*) and announced in its early evening edition that *Gone with the Wind* had won. The Academy changed its rule from that day forward to only allow winners to be named at the show.

The snow in *The Wizard of Oz*'s famous poppy-field scene was made of the far-from-wonderful material asbestos. For decades, asbestos-based fake snowflakes had been a popular Christmas decoration throughout the United States and Europe. It was sold in boxes and tossed liberally on Christmas trees and living rooms around the holidays—and was the go-to material for creating a snowy effect on film. It was a poisonous scheme that could have been devised by the Wicked Witch herself.

40

"**Jingle Bells**" was originally about Thanksgiving. The song was written in the mid-nineteenth century by James Pierpont, whom historians believe wrote it for the Thanksgiving program at his father's Sunday school. The song, copyrighted under the title "One Horse Open Sleigh," contains no reference to Christmas or December and only the mention of snow connects it to the holiday season (Pierpont, originally from Medford, Massachusetts, was inspired by the sleigh races that occurred there, but may have actually written the song while spending a snowless winter in Georgia, pining for his snowy home).

CHAPTER 2

Dracula, Bubonic Plague, and Knock-Knock Jokes

"*Truth is stranger* than fiction, but it is because Fiction is obliged to stick to possibilities; Truth isn't."

—*Mark Twain,*
FOLLOWING THE EQUATOR

41

Santa Claus was invented by Coca-Cola—at least our modern image of him. While depictions of St. Nicholas has varied through the centuries, it was the soft drink's national ad campaigns early in the twentieth century that gave the character his familiar red fur outfit, twinkling eyes, and huge gut. Prior to that, he was more likely to be thought of as the puckish "jolly old elf" described in Clement Clarke Moore's famous holiday poem, "A Visit from St. Nicholas." The appealing and widespread image developed by Coke and its advertising agency effectively brought the character into the modern era and has shaped our image of Santa Claus ever since.

42

Geoffrey Chaucer might be the person who made St. Valentine romantic. The canonized Roman man (or, according to some academics, pair of men who were combined to create the figure) known as St. Valentine did not have an especially love-filled backstory. The first references made to him as a romantic figure were in Chaucer's fourteenth-century poem "Parlement of Foules" about birds choosing their mates: "For this was on Seynt Valenynes day, / Whan every foul cometh ther to chese his make." The professor who presented this theory suggests that Chaucer may have connected the saint's day of February 14 to the spring (the season came earlier in Europe at the time), with its amorous associations of the birds and bees, or that he simply liked the sound of "Valentines." Whatever the reason, after its publication, the references to Valentine's Day as a time for romance quickly caught on.

43

Green is everywhere on St. Patrick's Day, but the figure was historically associated with the color blue. The Order of St. Patrick, an eighteenth-century order of chivalry in the Kingdom of Ireland, adopted a shade of sky blue that some academics believe was selected to distinguish it from England's royal blue. This became closely connected to the figure to the point that it became officially known as "St. Patrick's blue" (the Kingdom of Ireland itself was associated with a dark blue at the time). The connection with green likely came soon after that, as supporters of Irish independence adopted the color to support their cause. Green has been linked with the historic figure and the holiday ever since.

44

Instead of pumpkins, the people of England used to carve faces into turnips during the fall celebration that was the precursor to what Americans would develop into Halloween. The English would practice "souling," in which a candle set inside a carved turnip was meant to represent a soul in purgatory. Dressed in costume, they would go house-to-house with these turnip lanterns, asking for gifts of cakes and nuts and singing and playing music as they went. Americans adapted this practice using a pumpkin since it was more plentiful in North America.

46

Though he set the long opening section of *Dracula* in Transylvania, Bram Stoker never set foot in the region. In fact, the author never got further east than Vienna. He actually wrote much of his novel in the sunny English seaside town of Whitby, a popular holiday spot for British vacationers at the time. He filled in the details by drawing on travel books and written accounts, giving the average Victorian reader the impression he knew what he called "one of the wildest and least known portions of Europe" like the back of his hand.

47

$\mathscr{P}$art of the reason some of Charles Dickens' novels run so long is that he was paid for his writing by the word. Dickens' longer works were published in serial form, with eager readers looking forward to the next segment on a monthly or weekly basis—and he counted on the regular checks he received on the same schedule. To stretch his income, the beloved author admitted to friends that on at least a few occasions he had stretched out the action of his novels or added extra scenes in order to keep the money coming in. In one letter to a friend while Dickens was at work on *David Copperfield,* he wrote, "This one has grown far longer than I had intended—as long as my pages stack as high as my bills, all will be well."

48

James Joyce used crayons to write some of his novels. He composed much of *Ulysses* and *Finnegans Wake* on huge sheets of white paper. This not only made it possible for him to organize the notes for his long and complicated works, but allowed him to actually see them. Suffering from ocular disease late in life, Joyce was almost totally blind when he wrote *Finnegans Wake*. The great modernist author had a complicated system of writing and revising his work using blue, green, orange, and other colored crayons to cross through entries and notes as he incorporated them into his draft of the intricate novel.

49

Drinking was a cornerstone of Ernest Hemingway's writing process. He loved his martinis and famously once downed seventeen double daiquiris at Cuba's Floridita restaurant, but he was pretty much open to any alcohol—wine, beer, or spirit—and he claimed he was drunk throughout the writing of both *The Sun Also Rises* and *A Farewell to Arms*. That might explain why such a huge range of drinks appears in his novels and stories. Philip Greene, who wrote an entire cocktail book of drinks mentioned in Hemingway's writings, says "perhaps more than any other writer, he engaged his characters in the act of eating and drinking." Being drunk yourself while writing about them no doubt helps in that effort.

50

Edith Wharton was the first woman to win a Pulitzer Prize. In 1921, she received the prize for *The Age of Innocence*, her 1920 novel about Gilded Age New Yorkers, beating Sinclair Lewis' satire *Main Street* (he had initially been the committee's pick but lost due to the judges' concerns about the political nature of his book). While dubbed "The First Lady of Letters," Wharton was not able to repeat the trick with the Nobel Prize: while nominated for that award in 1927, 1928, and 1930, she would never actually win.

51

Edith Wharton also coined the phrase "keeping up with the Joneses." In her 1905 novel *The House of Mirth*, the narrator describes how the protagonist Lily Bart feels competitive among the glamour and refinement of New York City's high society, and in one scene describes how she must go shopping before a prominent ball in order to "keep up with the Percys, Dorsets, and Joneses."

52

T.S. Eliot is best known for heavy modernist poetry such as *The Waste Land*, but he was also a huge fan of practical jokes. He regularly pulled pranks on friends and family, giving them exploding cigars or seating them in chairs where he had secretly stashed a whoopee cushion. He adored Groucho Marx (who admired the poet in return) and the two struck up an epistolary friendship, communicating regularly by letters. But when they finally met in 1964, things did not go as smoothly as they might have hoped. While Marx was interested in enjoying a literary discussion with the author, Eliot cared only to discuss the comedian's 1933 comedy *Duck Soup*. No reports exist of whether Eliot may have also given the comedy legend the whoopee-cushion treatment.

53

Nineteenth-century newsboys invented the knock-knock joke. These scrappy youths made a living selling papers throughout major American cities, going door-to-door to drop off papers to subscribers and offering them a quick summary of the day's sensational headlines or entertaining them with a pun-heavy joke. These began as silly responses when the customer asked, "who's there?" and evolved into more elaborate call-and-response jokes hardly different from the typical knock-knock joke you are likely to hear today.

54

The expression "the whole nine yards" originally referred to the volume of a concrete mixer. The first rotating mixers held nine cubic yards (6.9m^2) of cement, so when a customer requested a full truckload of concrete, they would ask for "the whole nine yards." In construction, this grew to refer to any sizable job and eventually was applied to many other areas. Another theory was that the term originated with World War II fighter planes, whose belts of ammunition ran for nine yards. A pilot engaged in an intense battle that exhausted his ammo would be said to have used "the whole nine yards." The only trouble with this theory? The phrase never appeared in World War II literature and ammunition is measured in rounds, not by the length of the belt.

55

OMG is not as recent a term as you might think. The shorthand for "Oh My God" goes back at least a century, when it was used in an exchange with none other than future British Prime Minister Winston Churchill. In 1917, retired Admiral of the British Navy John Arbuthnot Fisher wrote to Churchill (then a British member of Parliament) about rumors he had heard about new titles that would soon be bestowed. "I hear that a new order of Knighthood is on the tapis," he wrote. "O.M.G. (Oh! My God!)—Shower it on the Admirality!!" Fisher would have, no doubt, been a fan of emojis as well.

56

The origin of the word "blackmail" has nothing to do with the mail. It actually derives from the Old Norse word *mál*, meaning "agreement." In the sixteenth century, English farmers living in Scotland were often extorted into giving up goods or money in order to avoid having their land pillaged. This underhanded, or "black," agreement led to it being dubbed "blackmail." In the latter half of the eighteenth century it evolved into its current meaning of demanding money in return for not revealing embarrassing information.

57

𝓐rchaeologists have uncovered a network of medieval tunnels that stretch thousands of miles, connecting from Scotland all the way to Turkey. This twelve-thousand-year-old system of tunnels likely served as a way for men to travel and transport supplies while protecting themselves from predators and the harsh elements aboveground. Rather than a direct road from Scotland to Turkey, it likely served more as a medieval railroad, where travelers could hop on or off at whatever stop they liked—Germany, Austria, Romania, or otherwise.

58

The oldest preserved human body in the world was covered in tattoos. Ötzi the Iceman, estimated to have lived about 5,300 years ago, and whose mummified body was discovered in the Alps along the Austrian-Italian border in 1991, sports no fewer than fourteen sets of tattoos from his lower back to his feet. His body was impressively preserved, allowing scientists to identify a small cross on his anklebone, a group of seven short lines around his left calf, and a vertical sets of lines on his back, likely made with soot. Okay, so the designs were not incredibly detailed, but you try inking a hummingbird with a 3000 BC tattoo needle.

59

*T*he term *on cloud nine* is rooted in Greek mythology. The Nephelai, also known as the cloud and rain nymphs, were believed to be a trio of beautiful robed sisters who were responsible for rainfall as well as cloud formations. In one myth, one of the nymphs grew infatuated with Uranus, the god of the sky. Her affections were at first unrequited and she watched him only from afar. But as her attraction grew, she climbed through one layer of heaven after another in an attempt to catch a closer look at him. When she finally reached the ninth level, Uranus noticed her and the two had a stormy romance. The joyful thrill the nymph experienced upon connecting with her beloved at the ninth level of heaven morphed into *on cloud nine* as an expression of intense excitement.

60

Scholars in the Middle Ages never actually believed the world was flat. They subscribed to the belief that the Earth was spherical, following theories going back to the Ancient Greeks. The myth that most people of this era believed the Earth was flat got started in the late 1800s as proponents of the theory of evolution sought to paint nonbelievers as akin to the flat-Earthers of earlier centuries, even if these flat-Earthers never really existed.

61

𝒯*he bubonic* plague killed an estimated fifty million people throughout Asia, Europe, and Africa, but almost exclusively affected the poor. The nasty infection, which resulted in swollen and burst lymph nodes and eventually death, ravaged medieval Europe, wiping out entire villages and families. But contemporary accounts show that, outside of a few scattered instances, wealthy merchants, prominent lords and ladies, and other noblemen were virtually untouched by the disease.

62

*T*hink the Black Death is ancient history? Not if you take the New York City subway. Researchers at Weill Cornell Medical College swabbed more than four hundred subway stations in the city and found strains of the bubonic plague—as well as anthrax, *Escherichia coli*, and gonorrhea. While it was not found in a high enough concentration to pose an immediate risk to subway riders, it was enough for the researchers to warn passengers to be sure to wash their hands every time they took mass transportation in the city.

63

Speaking of fearing public transportation, when the escalator was first introduced on the London Underground, a one-legged man proved just the salesman to put travelers' worries to rest. Executives at the escalator's manufacturer, Mowlem & Cochrane, tapped its Clerk of Works on Underground Projects, William "Bumper" Harris—who just happened to be missing a leg— to help demonstrate how safe the innovation was. He rode the first escalator to demonstrate that there was little chance of losing one's balance while getting on or off. Although some cynically suggested that the escalator might be to blame for taking Harris' limb in the first place, the pitch had its desired effect and soon Londoners were making stops specifically to test out the new invention.

64

Smoking has been illegal on all domestic United States flights for years, yet the Federal Aviation Administration requires that every plane lavatory be equipped with an ashtray—and if one of them is broken, the airline is required to report and replace them within three days. The reason for this is that, even though smoking is illegal, a handful of passengers are still likely to light up, nicotine addiction being what it is. It is far more dangerous for a passenger to dispose of their butt in the paper towel–filled trash, which could catch fire and imperil the entire plane. When that's the alternative, the occasional sneaky smoker who chucks his or her butt in the ashtray is a small price to pay.

65

𝒯𝒽𝑒 𝑓𝒾𝓇𝓈𝓉 time Amelia Earhart saw a plane, she was less than impressed. As a child at the Iowa State Fair in Des Moines in 1908, an adult pointed out an airplane to her, saying, "Look, dear, it flies." But Earhart saw only "a thing of rusty wire and wood," as she would later write in her memoirs. "I looked as directed but confess I was much more interested in an absurd hat made of an inverted peach-basket which I had just purchased for fifteen cents." Her opinion would change quite a bit as she got older.

66

Railroad companies created U.S. time zones. As railroads enabled passengers to cover hundreds of miles in a matter of hours, it became a nightmare for railroad operators to schedule stops using local times based on the sun's position (the way that clocks had traditionally been set). So, at exactly noon on November 18, 1883, the railroad companies established a set of four time zones across the United States and Canada, laying out divisions that are quite close to the time zone lines we still use today. Not until 1918 did Congress formally adopt these as our national time zones.

67

Very little of the Underground Railroad was actually underground. While the popular image of the routes used to usher fugitive slaves out of slaveholding states imagines the escapees being secreted through subterranean tunnels or hiding in cellars, basements, and clandestine closets, few homes actually had such secret passageways. As Henry Louis Gates, Jr., explains: "Most fugitive slaves spirited themselves out of towns under the cover of darkness, not through tunnels, the construction of which would have been huge undertakings and quite costly."

68

Those assisting with the Underground Railroad would create "freedom quilts" with coded messages alerting escaping fugitives of the location of safe houses and secure passages to reach the north. Hung from windows, the quilts were a way for sympathizers of abolition to assist without being detected and punished. The symbols could be elaborately complex, incorporating biblical images, animals, and more, in ways that would be picked up on by the escapees but fly under the radar of local authorities.

69

Harriet Tubman was a tough woman for many reasons—more than a dozen missions to help rescue slaves and the first woman to lead an armed expedition in the Civil War, to name two—but one of her most astonishing bits of bravery was receiving brain surgery with minimal anesthetic. In the late 1890s she went to Massachusetts General Hospital complaining of "achin' and buzzin'" in her head, as she described it in her autobiography, which her doctor suspected could be relieved by releasing pressure in her skull. She declined the anesthetic and "just lay down like a lamb before the slaughter, and he sawed open my skull, and raised it up." The only thing to help her get through the procedure? A bullet clenched between her teeth.

71

another way that efforts to ease discomfort went too far was with the creation and popularity of "soothing syrups." Also known as "infant's friends" and "colic cures," these medicines and lozenges sold during the late nineteenth century promised to calm upset babies and make the lives of new mothers much easier. Unfortunately, they also contained a battery of narcotics that an adult might think twice about ingesting, let alone a kid who was only a few months old. Upon investigating the remedies, the *New York Times* found that they contained chloroform, morphine hydrochloride, codeine, heroin, powdered opium, and far more. Parents soon decided that a crying baby was better than one hooked on morphine.

72

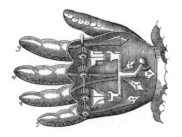

Hand transplants are not uncommon, and doctors have even successfully completed a number of double transplants—usually from a deceased donor to a person who has lost their hands. But there has been at least one case of a "cosmetic hand transplant." A thirty-seven-year-old man who had become fed up with his right hand, which he considered "ugly and veiny," found a doctor in São Paulo, Brazil, who removed the hand and swapped it with an unscarred one— for the bargain price of $11,500.72.

73

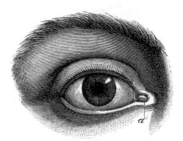

***O**ur eyes* are the same size for our entire lives. It may seem crazy, but the dimensions of our eyeballs at birth remain as such into adulthood. When you look at a baby's face, you are seeing mostly their irises and a small amount of the whites of their eyes. As a person ages, their face enlarges and more of their eyeballs become visible, making it seem that the organ is getting larger, but in fact it remains unchanged.

74

Just like irises or fingerprints, every person has a unique tongue print. Biometric scans can be done to compare the individual shape (long or short, wide or narrow) and texture (ridges, wrinkles, and marks) of the tongue. The tongue's attributes are recorded on a "tongue image-acquiring device," which captures tiny details and processes this information with specialized software that maps the tongue and compares it to others in a database. Even better, you don't have to lick an ink pad to record its pattern—just stick it out and you're set.

75

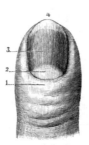

Our fingernails and hair continue to grow after we die—but not as long as is often reported. While nerve cells die about five minutes after death, skin cells (which produce nails) and hair matrix cells (which produce hair) take days to expire, allowing both fingernails and hair to continue growing at their usual rate of 0.004 inches (0.1mm) per day. Both will continue growing for two to six days after death—about one-half centimeter, give or take.

76

*K*nuckle cracking is not just an annoying habit; it may actually contribute to arthritis. The sound comes from releasing gas contained in the synovial fluid that acts as a lubricant between the bones of the knuckles. Repeatedly releasing this gas has been found to reduce the efficacy of the lubricating fluid, causing the bones to rub against each other without the protective layer working as well as it should. Over time, this can cause an inflammation of the joints, and scientists have found a correlation between sufferers of arthritis and habitual knuckle crackers—in case you needed another reason to quit this irritating behavior.

77

What we often refer to as "double jointed" is what physicians officially call "hypermobility" or "joint laxity"—defined as the ability to move one's joints farther than most people are able. And it's something you are born with, not something you can learn. For example, some people have a small olecranon—the knob of bone that forms the pointy part of the elbow—which allows them to hyperextend their elbows. While athletes and dancers may enhance their flexibility over years of training, they will not truly be "hypermobile." So if you're born with hypermobility, you've got a leg—or elbow—up on the competition.

78

S tatements like "we only use 10 percent of our brains" are nonsense. While it may be the case that we do not use every part of our brains simultaneously at all times, researchers using brain-imaging technology have found that most regions of the organ are active throughout the day. Even a task as routine as making a peanut butter sandwich involves a huge amount of neuronal activity. As you unscrew the jar, pick up a butter knife, decide how much peanut butter to put on the bread, and spread it, you are using occipital and parietal lobes, motor sensory and sensory motor cortices, cerebellum, frontal lobes, and plenty more.

79

W**hat's **one of the world's greatest dangers? Lack of sleep. Among the major disasters caused by sleep deprivation: the Chernobyl nuclear meltdown (the engineers involved had been working for more than thirteen hours straight); the *Exxon Valdez* oil spill (members of the crew had worked for twenty-two hours and took only a brief nap before having to get back to work); and the *Challenger* explosion (managers involved in the launch slept only two hours before reporting to work on the day of the disaster). Research backs this up. One study by Washington State University found that subjects who went without sleep for two days failed coordination, decision-making, and learning tests that well-rested subjects passed easily. So get your sleep!

80

The chemical tryptophan in turkey does not actually make you sleepy. A hearty Thanksgiving feast is reliably followed by a bout of drowsiness. And this is usually attributed to this amino acid which is a component of brain chemicals that help a person relax. But turkey contains just as much (or in some cases, less) tryptophan as other meats, soybeans, cheeses, and even sunflower seeds. If anything, that drowsiness you feel (formally known as "postprandial somnolence") is likely caused by the high-carb stuffing and mashed potatoes accompanying the turkey.

CHAPTER 3

Jet Lag, Jellyfish, and Cricket Ears

"**Whatever satisfies** the soul is truth."

—Walt Whitman

81

The best ways to beat jet lag: a red-eye flight and a few glasses of wine. Traveling at night is not only the best way to maximize your vacation time (who wants to blow a day of travel sitting on an airplane?), it also is an effective way to fight jet lag, since the "desynchronization" that happens when we travel across time zones is more quickly overcome while we sleep. Wine has also been found to both encourage drowsiness—even earlier in the evening when we wouldn't normally go to sleep—but helps speed up the "reset" of our biological clock when we land.

82

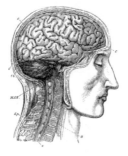

The concept of "right brain" versus "left brain" is based on physiological fact. The human brain is composed of two hemispheres, with the left managing analytical/logical tasks and the right engaged in creative/emotional work. Multiple studies have found that people tend to use one side more than the other—and those who activated their right brain more performed better on creative tasks while those using their left side achieved stronger results on analytical tasks. The differences come out in other ways as well: right-brained people prefer cats, rock music, and read mysteries, while left-brained people prefer dogs, classical music, and nonfiction.

83

*S**having your** hair* makes it grow back thicker —but only the first time. Dermatologists have found that when the hair on a portion of skin is shaved for the first time, the follicles grow back slightly denser than the hairs that had been removed. This may be a holdover from our caveman days when body hair was a necessity for staying warm and the body responded to its removal by trying to replenish it and then some. But this only works the first time: in subsequent shaves, the hair grows back just as thick.

84

Chewing your food longer can help you lose weight. Victorian health enthusiast Horace Fletcher devised a practice of chewing each bite thirty to seventy times (including milk and soup) and lost sixty pounds within five months. His slogan "Nature will castigate those who don't masticate" attracted adherents including Thomas Edison and John D. Rockefeller. Though his approach to health would fall out of popularity by the early twentieth century, recent studies have backed up his findings, including one by Chinese researchers stating that those who chew at least forty times per bite consumed about 12 percent fewer calories than those who chewed fifteen times per bite.

85

For those who felt mastication did not create the radical weight loss they sought, there was another solution in the early part of the twentieth century: tapeworms. The first decades of the 1900s saw a spate of quack remedies that offered tapeworms as their active ingredients. "Eat! Eat! Eat! And Always Stay Thin!," promised one ad, reading, "Fat, the ENEMY that is shortening Your Life, Banished! How? With Sanitized Tape Worms." Though these sold well for a few years, they eventually caught the attention of the Bureau of Chemistry of the United States Department of Agriculture (now the Food and Drug Administration), which investigated and shut down the sale of these pills.

86

You don't lose half your body's heat through your head—it's more like 90 percent. Your head expends a higher than average amount of energy since the skin is much thinner around your skull than around other parts of your body. On top of that, your scalp contains lots of blood vessels that sit close to the skin's surface. Thus an excess amount of heat escapes through the top of your head, making a wool hat a very worthwhile investment during cold months.

87

𝓦𝓮 𝓭𝓸 not have just five senses—in fact, we have at least ten, depending on who you ask. In addition to sight, smell, touch, taste, and hearing, humans also have "proprioception" *and* "nociception." The latter is our sense of pain, the former is the sense of space (for example, being able to touch your nose while closing your eyes, or switching from the gas to the brake pedal without looking at your feet). We also have "equilibrioception" (sense of balance), "thermoception" (sense of heat and cold), "temporal perception" (sense of time), and more. So, technically, being able to see dead people would be at least an eleventh sense.

88

Just as there are more than five senses, there are more than three states of matter. We all know solids, liquids, and gases, but there are two others which often get overlooked. The first is plasma—the most common state of matter in the universe—in which electrons move freely without being tethered to a nucleus (unlike in the three better-known forms of matter). The second is the (awkwardly named) Bose-Einstein condensates, which are created by cooling a group of atoms so close to absolute zero that molecular motion nearly stops and the atoms clump together.

89

$\mathcal{T}$*he animal* with the strongest sense of hearing is not a bat or a dolphin (which can hear from some high frequencies and huge distances), but a moth. The greater wax moth, also known as *Galleria mellonella*, has been found to have "the most extreme hearing" of any known species—detecting frequencies of up to 300kHz (humans can hear up to only about 20kHz). The likely reason they have developed such extreme skills? To evade their predator, the sharp-eared bat.

90

Crickets' ears are on their knees. Among the tiniest ears in the animal kingdom, the hearing organs of crickets, grasshoppers, and katydids are made up of three main parts that are embedded in each knee: a pair of eardrums, an "acoustic vesicle" (a fluid-filled tube, something like an uncoiled version of a human cochlea), as well as a tympanal plate (which works like our three ear bones). The eardrums capture sound vibration, the tympanal plate sends these vibrations into the auditory vesicle, and the sound waves travel through the creature's *crista acustica*, to which the insect responds. Bees have nothing on these creatures—the expression should have been "the crickets' knees."

91

Bats are actually blind, just as the saying goes. They rely on echolocation (the fancy term for their natural sonar) to navigate through caves and across vast terrain as they forage for food. Bats send ultrasound from their larynxes, which then echoes off surrounding trees, mountains, and landscape. Although this echolocation functions as well in pitch dark as on a bright sunny day, bats have no traditional sense of sight and their eyes serve little practical purpose—they can sense light levels, but more by the feeling of warmth on their skin than actual ability to see.

92

We think of John James Audubon, founder of the National Audubon Society, as a naturalist who loved birds so much that he captured their likeness in his paintings better than almost anyone else before or since. In fact, he also loved shooting them. "He achieved unequaled realism by using freshly killed models held in lifelike poses by wires," according to historian David Wallechinsky in his book *Significa*. He adds that Audubon in some cases killed a dozen birds for one painting.

93

*B*aby venomous snakes are deadlier than adults. Well, they are just as venomous, with their small mouths producing the same level of poison as adult counterparts, but *because* those mouths are small, they pack much more per square inch. Further, since they are still getting coordinated in the use of their deadly weapon, baby snakes often expend far more venom per bite, whereas wiser adult snakes conserve their poison. It's the little ones you should watch out for.

94

Jellyfish can still sting after they are dead. For example, in 2010, a group of more than one hundred swimmers in New Hampshire were stung by the pieces of a dead, forty-pound carcass of a lion's mane jellyfish (which one zoologist described as similar to "loose spaghetti"). The tentacles can emit toxins even when dead or broken off the animal itself. As if poisonous jellyfish were not scary enough, you can add "zombie poisonous jellyfish" to your list of nightmares.

95

Speaking of jellyfish stings, urinating on them can actually make it hurt worse. Though the myth has persisted (through outdated books and reruns of *Friends*) that urine neutralizes the stinging cells of the venomous creature, this has not been replicated in actual lab tests. Scientists have found that applying urine—or ammonia or alcohol—to a sting has in fact done the opposite, causing active cells to fire, making it more painful. The thing that does work to lessen the pain? Household vinegar.

96

Camels can contain as much as thirteen gallons of water inside their humps. Scientists believe the built-in water tanks evolved as the desert-based creature was forced to travel far from natural water sources for days on end. The water allows them to survive with no hydration for seven days, and in some cases longer, though this can vary by elevation (camels at higher altitudes can go longer than those lower down). Think of them as nature's canteen.

97

They say that sex changes a person, and that's doubly true of prairie voles. When a male vole copulates, the animal's brain is actually changed. Prior to intercourse, it sees all females as identical and difficult to distinguish (though they can tell the difference between them and other males). Once the vole mates, the blinders come off and it is able to recognize the distinct smell, appearance, and behavior of individual females—and shows distinct preference to its partner. Scientists believe this is an adaptation that may help them to be better partners or fathers, as the vole is one of the few mammals that practices monogamy.

98

Ostriches do not bury their heads in the sand. Despite the popular image of the hefty bird diving face-first into the dirt when it's frightened, the creature's usual defensive strategy is to play dead—flopping to the ground and laying still, with neck and head laid out flat (which from a distance could appear like it's buried). But ostriches are no wimps. When it or its eggs are threatened, this big bird is just as likely to attack predators with a kick of its clawed foot—a thrust powerful enough to kill a lion.

99

Female lions do most of the hunting for their prides. The males do not move as quickly and tend to serve more as defenders of the pride, fighting off predators or killing prey that comes close. It's the agile lionesses that do the serious hunting and gathering, tracking down gazelle, zebra, giraffe, and anything else that they may spot, often working in teams and at night.

100

Giraffes sleep an average of thirty minutes a day. Because of their size and lack of thick hides or sharp teeth to fight predators, the long-necked mammals must remain alert as much as possible in case they need to make a run for it. When they do sleep, it's for about five minutes at a time and often with one eye open. That's truly a power nap.

101

Piranhas aren't nearly as dangerous as they are reputed to be. In fact, many are vegetarians, such as Brazil's *Tometes camunani*, which survives on riverweeds only. Attacks on humans and large mammals are rare: in most cases in which they've actually eaten human flesh, the person had been dead already. In the few cases where they have attacked a swimmer, it's been a single bite per victim, rather than the swarm that movies would have you believe. Scientists maintain that, like bears, they generally keep to themselves unless they or their eggs are attacked. So if you find yourself in piranha-infested water, chances are good that you'll survive.

102

Not one, but *two* presidents received alligators as White House guests. Long before our nation had animal rights organizations, some exotic animals took up residence at the White House. French general Georges Washington de La Fayette gave an alligator to John Quincy Adams when he visited the residence (he kept it in the unfinished East Room and the adjacent bathtub). And Herbert Hoover's son, Allan, had a pair of pet alligators who joined him on occasional visits to the White House. No doubt they kept the Secret Service on their toes.

103

Not content with the traditional dog or cat, William Howard Taft kept a pair of sheep, which grazed on the front of the White House lawn. Named Mooley and Wooly, the two were sheared each year and their wool was used for scarves and slippers for the Taft children or the occasional special guest to the White House.

104

The White House was originally gray. The president's residence was first completed in Washington, DC, in 1800, and the Aquia Creek sandstone used to construct it was a light gray color. The building's architect, James Hoban, left the structure this natural color, a common practice in the neoclassical design that was in vogue during this era. The building did not get its eponymous color until after British forces burned part of it during the War of 1812, requiring a significant rebuild. To help give it an added freshness, it was also painted the familiar bright white—the color it continues to be today.

105

Waffles, olive oil, and ice cream were all introduced to the United States by Thomas Jefferson. During the five years that the Founding Father spent as American minister to France, he developed quite a taste for the Parisian culinary scene. He ordered his nineteen-year-old chef (and slave), James Hemings, to learn French cooking and to teach it to the kitchen staff back in Monticello. Hemings did just that, becoming fluent in French and French cuisine. Upon returning to Virginia and later as president, Jefferson hosted elaborate dinner parties with French dishes prepared by Hemings and those he taught.

106

There was one thing Jefferson failed to bring to the United States: wine. Though a huge fan of vino from his time in France, during which he toured vineyards in Burgundy, Bordeaux, and beyond, his efforts to cultivate grapes in his home country went nowhere. American pests and diseases, as well as inhospitable soil, proved too much for his efforts to create a homegrown wine industry. But two centuries later, with the help of European winegrowers who helped Virginians rethink the varietals they were growing, the Virginia wine scene is booming (including at Jefferson Vineyards).

107

While John Hancock famously had the largest signature on the Declaration of Independence, Thomas Jefferson's was the largest signature on the Constitution. He made such a show of the signature that other Founding Fathers, including his longtime rival Alexander Hamilton, scoffed at his elaborate cursive as an attempt to garner the attention Hancock earned, even though the risks of signing the Constitution were far lower than those for severing the colonies from British rule.

108

The Founding Fathers did not sign the Declaration of Independence on the Fourth of July. While the Continental Congress formally agreed to break from the British on July 2, 1776, and it was formally adopted on July 4, most of the delegates didn't get around to signing it until August 2, 1776.

109

$\mathcal{T}$*he Pledge* of Allegiance originally ended "with liberty, justice, and happiness for all." When the United States entered World War I, it was believed that the last word was inappropriate for the country in the midst of war, especially considering the sacrifices made by the other European countries embroiled in it. In the 1920s, there was a brief effort to add "happiness" back into the pledge, but once it was out, it stayed out.

110

For a period, there were fifteen stripes on the American flag. Though the official American flag now carries only thirteen, reflecting the country's thirteen original colonies, at the time Vermont (1791) and Kentucky (1792) were admitted into the Union, the number of stripes was increased to fifteen. As it quickly became outdated when Tennessee (1796), Ohio (1803), and Louisiana (1812) joined the United States, the stripes held at fifteen. Finally, in 1818, President James Monroe, perhaps realizing that the number of states was only going to grow, set the number permanently at thirteen.

111

Abraham Lincoln is the only president to hold a U.S. patent. He invented a "manner of buoying vessels" that earned him U.S. patent number 6,469 in 1849. His idea was to equip the boat with rubber bellows that could be inflated should it hit a sandbar or similar snag, allowing the vessel to clear the obstacle and continue on its way (there's probably an analogy here to getting a bill through Congress). He received it while practicing law in Springfield, Illinois, even creating a wooden model of the device, whittling it at his law office and getting assistance from a local mechanic—though he never got a chance to test it. Apparently he had more important things to worry about.

112

Leonardo da Vinci invented an early form of scissors. Though most famous for his paintings, da Vinci was an active inventor, drawing up detailed plans for musical instruments, pumps, flying machines, and more, many of which were never actually constructed. But one of his eccentric ideas has proved enormously important: in 1503 he drew what he simply called "cutting tool." The hand-operated instrument, with two blades pivoting on a bolt, was soon adopted by tailors and manufacturers throughout Europe. It's a significant legacy, often overshadowed by his great artistic accomplishments.

113

Charles Darwin invented the office chair. At least, he is one of the first people known to add wheels to his chair, allowing him to move between his writing and numerous specimens with ease. The author of *On the Origin of Species* worked constantly and sought ways to do so as efficiently as possible. Adding wheels to his chair did just that. The innovation did not immediately catch on, however. It would take the growth of clerical work during the second half of the nineteenth century to spur the mass production and adoption of wheeled chairs that would become a staple of every American office. Evolution takes time.

114

americans are the only people who use no. 2 pencils. The number indicates the hardness of the pencil's graphite, on a scale of 1 to 4, with the higher number indicating a harder core. The softer the pencil (a result of a lower proportion of clay in the graphite) the lighter its mark on the paper. But if you picked up a pencil anywhere outside of the United States, you would see letters instead of (or in addition to) numbers: "H" indicates the hardness of the pencil, "B" refers to its blackness, and "F" to the fact that it sharpens to a fine point. So a pencil marked "HHBBB" or "2H3B" is very hard and very black. It's enough to make one appreciate the clear simplicity of the basic "no. 2."

115

Nasa spent about $5 million developing a pen that works in space. In the 1960s, as the space race heated up, the government organization faced a challenge: since ballpoint pens rely on gravity in order to put ink to paper, writing in space was virtually impossible. They spent several million dollars (of taxpayer money) commissioning a number of engineers and manufacturers to figure out how it could be done. After three years of trial and error, Paul C. Fisher of the Fisher Pen Company developed a solution. His patented space pen was able to write upside down and in extreme weather conditions, down to -50 degrees Fahrenheit and up to 400 degrees Fahrenheit. The Soviets, in the meantime, found a less expensive solution: they just used a common wooden pencil.

116

*B*oth Presidents Jimmy Carter and Ronald Reagan believed in UFOs. Carter filed two formal reports while governor of Georgia—to the UFO Bureau in Oklahoma and the National Investigations Committee on Aerial Phenomena—describing having seen a red and green orb in the sky outside Leary, Georgia. During a Southern Governors Conference, Carter stated that "I don't laugh at people any more when they say they've seen UFOs. I've seen one myself." Reagan described his own experience, in a plane outside Bakersfield, California: "I looked out the window and saw this white light. It was zigzagging around…I said to [the pilot]….'Let's follow it!'"

117

Dwight D. Eisenhower was pleased with the Soviet Union's launch of *Sputnik*. While the popular perception is that the 1957 launch of the first artificial Earth satellite—by the United States' Cold War enemy—angered the American administration and caught it off-guard, the opposite was true. While the public was shocked by the launch and the advanced stage of the Soviet program, Eisenhower and his team had long been aware of the country's capabilities (thanks to U-2 spy plane photos) and were not overly concerned with *Sputnik*'s launch. What did concern them were the questions about the legality of space and whether other countries could dispute the United States' right to such a satellite, or even shoot it down. By going first, the USSR protected the United States from having to pioneer this new field of international—or rather, interplanetary—law.

118

The Soviet Union banned microwaves. After a three-year research effort in 1976, scientists in the USSR determined that the electromagnetic field created by the (at the time still novel) technology was dangerous to those who used the appliances. They concluded that "use of these microwaves presents significant health risks to our citizens, sapping energy and increasing the risk of disease." Though regulators were not specific about what "disease" the microwaves caused, the concern was strong enough for the appliances to be prohibited for almost a decade until Perestroika and an effort to encourage free trade with the West led them to loosen restrictions.

119

There are higher levels of abnormal behavior during full moons. Belief in this phenomenon goes back centuries—it's where the words *lunacy* and *lunatic* come from and the reason why, in eighteenth-century England, people convicted of murder got lighter sentences if the crime occurred during a full moon. But there is also scientific support for this: a number of meta-analyses of research on the "lunar effect" on individuals' behavior found a consistent correlation between the lunar cycle and human behavior, with higher levels of strange as well as criminal behavior taking place when the full moon was up.

CHAPTER 4

Outhouses, Oreos, and Niagara Falls

"**Those are** the facts. But the facts can obscure the truth . . ."
—*Maya Angelou*

120

If you are looking to get pregnant, your best chance to conceive may be during a full moon. Decades of census data in the United States and throughout the world have found a consistent pattern of higher rates of conception when the moon is full. As it happens, a similar parallel is found between birth rates and full moons, with a higher level of children than average being born when the moon is fully illuminated. Although a correlation is clear, scientists have yet to find a specific physiological reason why.

121

It seems logical to assume the planet closest to the sun would also be the hottest. Although Mercury is the former, it is not the latter. While Mercury is plenty warm, with a maximum temperature of about 800 degrees Fahrenheit, it's only the second-hottest planet. The hottest is Venus, which reaches temperatures of 863 degrees Fahrenheit, despite being further from the sun than Mercury. The reason: Venus has a very thick atmosphere that traps the sun's heat, whereas Mercury has barely any atmosphere and releases the heat immediately. This is compounded by Venus' reflective clouds (and Mercury's lack of them), which further help hold in the hot.

122

The Great Wall of China is not actually visible from space—at least by the naked eye. The rumor that it was the only man-made structure visible from space, or even from the moon, began at least as far back as 1938. While the wall is indeed huge, it is made from materials similar in color and texture as the surrounding land, making it even tougher to spot, even in magnified photos. As *Apollo 12* astronaut Alan Bean explained: "The only thing you can see from the moon is a beautiful sphere, mostly white, some blue and patches of yellow, and every once in a while some green vegetation."

123

Lightning often strikes more than one place when it hits. NASA-funded researchers recorded almost four hundred lighting flashes one summer in Tucson, Arizona, and found that 35 percent of them struck the ground in two or more places that were separated by 32 feet (10m) or more. On average, each flash struck the ground in 1.45 places. In other words, you have a greater risk of getting struck by lightning than conventional wisdom might have you believing.

124

Lightning also strikes the same place more than once—sometimes in the same night. For example, on the night of June 30, 2014, Chicago was hit by a huge lightning storm, with some three hundred strikes within fifteen minutes—ten of which hit the Willis Tower (formerly the Sears Tower), eight hit Trump Tower, and four struck the John Hancock Center. In a year, the Willis Tower is hit by lighting as many as one hundred times.

125

The crescent moon on outhouses indicated it was for women. The semicircle-shaped symbol cut into the door of a wooden outhouse is a common sight in Western films full of manly men doing manly things. But it is believed to have originally been intended to alert women that this was the restroom for their use (likely signifying Luna or the goddess Diana) while a star or full circle (representing the sun sign Sol) was meant for men—early versions of the "woman" and "man" symbols on bathrooms today. Those tavern owners and innkeepers who could only be bothered to maintain one outhouse would generally opt for one with a moon, since men could use a nearby tree to meet their needs, and soon the moon became standard.

126

The bathroom scene in Alfred Hitchcock's *Psycho* was shocking to audiences—but not just because of all the murder. It was the first film to show a toilet being flushed. At the time it was considered inappropriate to show a toilet being used in film, and that's just what Hitchcock did: presenting a scrap of paper, which proves an important clue, failing to flush. In the book, the clue was an earring found in the bathroom, but Hitchcock changed it to a piece of paper actually *in* the toilet partly to add an extra jolt for viewers.

127

S*peaking of* breaking taboos, the first couple shown in bed together on prime-time television were Fred and Wilma Flintstone. Prior to that, TV couples from Lucy and Ricky in *I Love Lucy* to Rob and Laura on *The Dick Van Dyke Show* were always depicted in separate beds. The writers of *The Flintstones* were less skittish about these social rules, likely because it was a cartoon, and they were shown in bed in the show's first season, which aired in 1960. Soon live-action shows followed suit.

128

Fred Rogers, the host of *Mister Rogers' Neighborhood,* was once a Navy SEAL. Helping to teach kids about friendship and kindness to children was a piece of cake compared to the intense training he went through to serve as part of this elite division of the U.S. Navy. He never saw combat (enlisting just after World War II ended), but he completed the entire eighteen-month training regimen and served in the navy for years before returning to civilian life. He later credited his service with instilling in him an appreciation of individual character and the importance of passing these lessons onto the younger generation—not to mention his preternatural calmness. Look closely and you can see some bulging muscles under those mild-mannered sweaters.

129

One thing that deeply frightened Victorians was being buried alive. Widespread fear of premature burial led them to devise elaborate safeguards so that the newly buried could send an alert if they were actually alive. The most famous of these was "Bateson's Belfry," a bell mounted to the top of the coffin, with a string connecting to a finger of the (supposedly) deceased. If the person woke, they could wiggle their finger and help would come running to save them. Inventor George Bateson devised the contraption, patenting it as the "Bateson Life Revival Device" and earning him a small fortune as well as the Order of the British Empire from Queen Victoria herself.

130

Aldous Huxley and C.S. Lewis died the same day. It might have been a shock to lose two major literary figures in such quick succession if it weren't for the fact that another event commanded the day's headlines: the death of John F. Kennedy. Huxley died at 5:20 p.m., London time, and Lewis died about ten minutes later. But just under an hour after that, before the news of their deaths even broke, JFK was assassinated in Dallas, Texas. When asked how Lewis would have felt about being eclipsed by Kennedy, the Chronicles of Narnia author's stepson said he would have appreciated that his family could enjoy the privacy granted by the world's attention being directed elsewhere.

131

$\mathcal{T}$**hough William** Shakespeare wrote *Richard III* more than one hundred years after its namesake's death, his physical descriptions of the king proved almost exact. When Richard III of England's bones were uncovered in 2012, they reflected a man with a huge hunchback who is "rudely stamp'd" and "deformed, unfinish'd," who cannot "strut before a wanton ambling nymph."

132

William **Shakespeare** wrote his own epitaph to ward off grave robbers. He died on April 23, 1616, at the age of fifty-two (by at least one account, after a night of hard drinking with fellow writers Ben Jonson and Michael Drayton). His remains were interred in the Church of the Holy Trinity in Stratford-upon-Avon, and over his tomb was engraved the Bard's warning to any would-be thieves: "Good friend, for Jesus' sake forbeare, / To dig the dust enclosed here. Blessed be the man that spares these stones, / And cursed be he that moves my bones." The curse seems to be working, as the bones are still there.

133

At least five men are entombed in the Hoover Dam. This massive public works project took more than five years to complete and resulted in the deaths of ninety-six men (and that's just the men who died at the site as a result of blasting, rock slides, or falling from the canyon walls—not including those who died of heat, illness, or natural causes). The workers put tremendous effort into recovering the bodies of lost crew members, but in at least five cases this became impossible—due to the body's location or inability of the workers to find them. Their remains are buried inside the concrete of the dam to this day.

134

The Taj Mahal is arguably the most ornate mausoleum ever built—except for the grave itself. Constructed to honor Mumtaz Mahal, the third (and favorite) wife of India's Shah Jahan, the architectural wonder took more than twenty years to complete and several fortunes to finance. Every inch of the forty-two-acre (170km²) complex exudes opulence, from the white marble inlaid with semiprecious stones to the calligraphy that lines the walls—all a tribute to the Shah's beloved. But the bodies of Mumtaz and Jahan themselves are housed in a comparatively plain crypt on a level below the Taj Mahal's main chamber. Muslim law prohibits the decoration of graves, which it characterizes as offensive vanity, so at least a few feet of this architectural wonder are understated.

135

The Brooklyn Bridge was once home to a Cold War fallout shelter. In 2006, city workers conducting a routine inspection of the iconic bridge stumbled upon a small room hidden in a dark vault in its arched masonry foundations. Stocked with medical supplies, blankets, water drums, and an estimated 352,000 crackers (which pack a high number of calories), it provided enough supplies to survive for weeks—though the likelihood that the masonry would have withstood a nuclear blast is doubtful. The most extraordinary part: fifty years after someone placed them in there, the crackers were still edible.

136

The keystone at the very top of the Gateway Arch in St. Louis, Missouri, holds a time capsule. The metal box, which was permanently welded in this spot on October 28, 1965, contains 762,000 signatures, many from students who were attending St. Louis schools at the time and which cover seven bundles of paper. As the final piece was put in place, the chair of the building committee told the crowd gathered at the dedication, "Children, when they grow up and have their own families, will be able to point to the Arch and say their names are in it."

137

Mount Everest is the highest mountain in the world, but it is not the tallest. That distinction goes to Hawaii's Mauna Kea volcano, which measures 33,476 feet (10,203.5m) from its base to its top. Mount Everest measures only 29,035 feet (8,849.9m) So why does Everest get all the attention? Much of Mauna Kea is underwater, with just 13,796 feet (4,205m) rising above sea level. The mountain has a few other distinctions: it is home to Lake Waiau, one of the highest lakes in the world. It is also believed to be one of the best places in the world to view the night sky, thanks to its extremely dry atmosphere, and researchers from throughout the world have telescopes operating from its summit. It is also the only place in Hawaii where visitors can go snowboarding year-round (as long as you don't mind getting to the top without a lift).

138

The Grand Canyon is both the world's deepest and longest canyon. At 277 miles (445.8km) long (not to mention 18 miles (29km) wide at some points), the twisting river valley is by far the longest on Earth. But perhaps more impressive is how far down it goes, reaching depths of an average of 1 mile (1.6km). Getting to the bottom takes an average of four to five hours, according to the National Park Service, which adds that "oddly enough, very few people ask how long the return hike will take." The answer: almost twice as long as the way down—an average of seven to eight hours—and, also according to the National Park Service, "Underestimating the elevation change and not eating or drinking enough can easily add a few hours to those averages."

139

Niagara Falls has been producing electricity since the late nineteenth century. The Niagara Falls Hydraulic Power & Manufacturing Company spent two decades constructing a canal for hydraulic power before it began operating in Niagara Falls, New York. The plant could produce a modest amount of electricity, generating direct current that could only be distributed as far as two miles. But it has expanded significantly since then, thanks to the opening of the Niagara Power Plant (since renamed the Robert Moses Niagara Hydroelectric Power Station) in 1961. Today the landmark generates 2.4 million kilowatts of power, making it one of the largest hydroelectric power plant in the United States.

140

The Great Pacific Garbage Patch, discovered in 1997, is a mass of floating debris discarded by the people of North America and Asia in the middle of the Pacific Ocean, kept spinning in place by circular ocean currents. Because this trash vortex is so far from any coast, no individual country will take responsibility for it (not that they could do much if they tried—a 2014 drone expedition of the patch concluded that there was one hundred times more plastic by weight than previously estimated, as well as permanent plastic islands measuring 50 feet (15.24m) and longer. The Garbage Patch is there to stay.

141

We usually think of lakes and rivers as ranging from blue to green in color, but some are naturally pink, red, and even spotted. The high level of salt in Lake Hillier in Western Australia has proven hospitable to halobacteria, helping give the body of water a hot-pink color reminiscent of a bottle of Pepto Bismol. The Spotted Lake, in the small town of Osoyoos in British Columbia, Canada, is packed with minerals including calcium and sodium sulphates that create small mineral pools as the water evaporates in warmer months—resulting in the otherworldly spots floating upon the water's surface. Fans of gory movies will want to check out Blood Falls, Antarctica, whose high level of iron-rich brine deep beneath the glacier give this frozen waterfall the bloody scarlet color that earns its name. It's enough to make a clear blue lake appear positively boring.

142

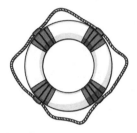

The owners and builders of the *Titanic* never claimed it was "unsinkable." While the legend (and a certain film) would have you believe that many boastful claims were made about the famous ship's invulnerability, this turns out to be a case of revisionist history. The White Star Line never stated that the ship's system of bulkheads and emergency doors made the vessel any more impervious to puncture or submersion than its other ships, and even media coverage of the ship made little mention of this particular aspect. As historian Richard Howells explains, "the population as a whole were unlikely to have thought of the *Titanic* as a unique, unsinkable ship before its maiden voyage."

143

The largest earthquake to hit the United States struck just a few decades ago. At 5:36 p.m. on March 27, 1964, a 9.2-magnitude quake detonated about seventy-five miles east of Anchorage, Alaska. Tsunamis, avalanches, and landslides—as well as eleven aftershocks—resulted, devastating towns in the region and killing 139 people. Ground fissures cut through Anchorage streets and sections of Alaska Railroad tracks were uprooted. As much destruction as this caused, it paled in comparison to the *worst* earthquake to ever hit Earth, which hit about 100 miles off the coast of Chile just four years earlier: the 9.5-magnitude quake parallel to the city of Valdivia, which destroyed some twenty thousand homes and killed as many as six thousand people.

144

laska was also on the receiving end of the world's biggest tsunami. At a height of 1,720 feet (524.3m; that's just a few dozen feet shy of the new One World Trade Center in New York City), the giant tsunami was caused by an 8.0-magnitude earthquake and resulting landslide in Lituya Bay—a quiet fjord near the Gulf of Alaska—on July 9, 1958. Forty million cubic yards of rock fell 3,000 feet, displacing huge amounts of water from the bay, creating the monster wave. But despite its size, the 1958 tsunami's death toll was thankfully low: it sank just one fishing boat, killing two men who were aboard.

145

The superstition against opening an umbrella indoors is relatively new, originating in eighteenth-century England. The metal-spoked umbrellas of the era could be ungainly and open at unpredictable moments. The awkwardness and occasional injury caused by these old-fashioned umbrellas discouraged members of London society from opening them indoors, and the practice evolved into a full-blown superstition.

146

The belief that throwing salt over one's shoulder can banish bad luck was actually invented by Benjamin Franklin. While we think of it as an ancient superstition, it was the Founding Father who popularized the concept, writing in his bestselling autobiography that "I'd learned from my Mother that bad luck could be countered with a pinch of Salt over the shoulder, generally the left." Soon after the publication of the book in 1791, references to the practice began to spread, but Franklin's was the first.

147

For decades, forks were viewed as not just a novelty, but sacrilege. In Tuscany during the eleventh century (when small forks were first used for eating, rather than as pitchforks), religious leaders spoke out against the use of the tools. They urged that people simply do what they'd done for centuries: use three fingers—thumb, index, and middle, keeping the pinkie and ring finger clean—and warned that using an artificial instrument was an offense to God. It probably did not help that forks at the time had only two tines, suspiciously resembling devil's horns.

148

While Italians had reservations about forks, the Chinese were uncomfortable with knives at the dining table. This is traced to the teachings of philosopher (and vegetarian) Confucius who urged that the sharp implements be left in the kitchen. As his follower Mencius put it, the superior man "keeps away from his slaughter-house and cook-room." The knife was a reminder of both these places and carried with it implications of violence and warfare. Thankfully, Asian cuisine developed just the tool to enjoy a meal without the need for sharp knives: chopsticks.

149

The word dessert comes from "de-serving" the table. Originally *desservir* in France, to which the earliest reference is in a health manual titled *Naturall and Artificial Directions for Health*, this part of the meal began as a simple palate cleanser after the table had been cleared and hands washed. Rather than the elaborate ice cream sundaes or slices of cake to which Americans have become partial, and which require a whole set of additional plates to be set, the original version of dessert was closer to the mint we receive at the end of our meals today.

150

During the Middle Ages, instead of using a platter to serve a large meal, it was common to use a "trencher"—a dense, flat, often stale round of bread on which the food would be set directly and passed from one person to the next. It soaked up any sauces and made cleanup a snap (typically the bread would be given as alms to the poor or tossed to the dogs nearby, or in some cases the guests themselves would share it).

151

artificial flowers used to be considered much more elegant than real ones. When French elites from the Middle Ages to the late eighteenth century sought a centerpiece or decorations for the table, "flowers could be thought rustic, not 'cultured' enough," according to historian Margaret Visser. Instead, they much preferred "silk, feather, cut-vegetable and other hand-made flowers, and reveled in their artificiality." An appreciation for real flowers as a table setting did not take hold until the nineteenth century.

152

Scientists are hard at work creating a better ketchup bottle. Specifically, they're developing a coating that creates super-slippery surfaces, allowing the ketchup to slide out more easily, creating a "completely emptyable bottle." The secret lies in imitating the lotus leaf—a hydrophobic surface that repels water more effectively than almost any other material through its surface of microscopic air pockets. These pockets reduce surface tension and send the water droplet on its way.

153

That "57" on Heinz bottles refers to pickles. The company was founded by Henry J. Heinz in 1869 as a pickle- and horseradish-preserving company—until it went bankrupt in 1875. Henry's brother and cousin resurrected the brand and expanded it to sell pickled cauliflower, sweet pickles, pickled onions, and plenty of non-pickled products (baked beans, tomato soup, and even apple butter). With this newly expanded product line, they adopted the slogan "57 Varieties." Ketchup was among these offerings and broke out as a bestseller once the company created its patented octagonal ketchup bottle. As Heinz has gone on to sell more than one billion ounces a year of the tomato-based condiment and acquired dozens of new brands and products, the "57" remains a standard part of the label.

154

The next time you are about to bite into an Oreo cookie, take a closer look at that design. The intricate pattern of triangles, lines, and dots on the wafers are more than just an appealing visual. The food scientist who invented the cookie was believed to be a Freemason and was interested in the medieval Knights Templar. He incorporated much of those organizations' symbolism into the pattern: The dashes, dots, and "flowers" are believed to represent the three degrees of Ancient Craft Masonry. The way the dots are placed on the cookie forms a five-point star (a common symbol of the organizations). The flowers on the wafer were also rendered using the Knights Templar "cross pattée"—a version of the Christian cross with a narrow center that fares out at the four tips. And you'll never guess what the cream represents.

155

Shopping carts, those vehicles of convenience for customers everywhere, were not very popular when first introduced. Sylvan Goldman, owner of a chain of Humpty-Dumpty grocery stores in the South, struck on the idea of a wheeled cart as he noticed shoppers ended their trip once their handheld baskets grew too heavy to lug around. He added wheels to a folding chair and attached a pair of metal baskets to it and offered them to shoppers. Few people took him up on the innovation, so he hired "decoy shoppers" whom he paid to wheel the carts around the store, demonstrating to customers how they could be used. That proved effective: a few people followed the model shoppers' example, then many others. It would become an international hit, with Goldman ending up with a $400 million fortune when he finally passed away in 1984.

156

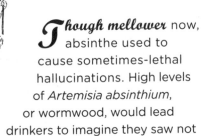

Though mellower now, absinthe used to cause sometimes-lethal hallucinations. High levels of *Artemisia absinthium*, or wormwood, would lead drinkers to imagine they saw not only green fairies, but "entire mystical lands populated with emerald-colored elves, ogres, and pixies," as one late-nineteenth-century account described. It was like living in *The Wizard of Oz*—until drinkers began dying. They suffered not from alcohol poisoning, but dehydration: so consumed would drinkers be in the fantasy world that they would forget to drink water. This led to the spirit being banned in the United States and most European countries until recently, when the recipe was modified.

157

The worm at the bottom of a bottle of mezcal is actually an aphrodisiac. Researchers have found that the addition of the worm (actually a caterpillar known as the *gusano*) changes the chemistry of the liquid in which it's immersed. Bottles containing a worm have a higher level of cis-3-Hexen-1-ol—an unsaturated alcohol that "has been recognized as a pheromone involved in mechanisms and behaviors of attraction in diverse animals such as insects and mammals," as one researcher put it. So drink up and your love life may blossom.

158

During Prohibition, the United States poisoned alcohol to discourage people from drinking it. They would "denature" industrial alcohol (the only kind that was legal at the time), adding iodine, zinc, mercury salts, formaldehyde, chloroform, and even gasoline and kerosene to make it not just disgusting, but deadly. But officials underestimated citizens' determination to get drunk and many Americans drank the stuff, anyway. In late 1926, soon after the policy was implemented, ill drinkers were suddenly showing up at hospitals and turning up dead. By some estimates, this poisoning of the alcohol led to the deaths of more than 10,000 people.

159

𝒯*he Bloody* Mary was originally known as a "Bucket of Blood." Invented at Harry's New York Bar (which was confusingly located in Paris) by bartender Ferdinand "Pete" Petiot, the mix of vodka and seasonings was introduced in 1920. American entertainer and Harry's patron Roy Barton was the one who dubbed it "Bucket of Blood," after a nightclub in Chicago. Perhaps because of the name, the drink did not catch on—until Petiot was brought to New York City's King Cole Bar, at the St. Régis Hotel, where he resurrected the recipe, rebranded as the "Red Snapper." By the late 1930s it was finally being called the "Bloody Mary," and the name stuck.

160

There is a bar that straddles the United States–Canada border, with part of the bar on both sides. Called the Borderline, it's half in the city of Derby Line, Vermont, and half in the city of Stanstead, Quebec, located in a historic building that allows it exemption from a number of international taxation rules. A line is drawn across the bar to indicate where one country ends and the other begins and its cocktail menu includes signature drinks such as the Border Hopper, Canada and Coke, and the War of 1812.

CHAPTER 5

High Heels, Hokey Pokey, and Piggy Banks

※—◆—※

"**A truth that's** told with bad intent/
Beats all the lies you can invent."

—**William Blake,**
"AUGURIES OF INNOCENCE"

161

Tags reading "Do not remove under penalty of law" were initially put on pillows due to a quirky Prohibition-era crime. When the sale of alcohol went underground after the United States outlawed it, bootleggers would slice open the seams of pillows (as well as couches, sofas, and other stuffed furniture) and store bottles of contraband inside them. The built-in padding and lack of regulation of stuffed furniture made this an ideal vehicle for moonshine, gin, and more. The federal government soon caught wind of this practice and put greater regulations on the sale and use of pillows, including prosecuting any consumers found to have tampered with them.

162

Scientists are researching a chemical that can quickly reduce the alcohol level in a person's blood—effectively creating a "sober pill." So far they have only been able to reduce blood alcohol level in mice, which they inject with specific enzymes that help process the alcohol. One of the researchers described it as "like having millions of liver cell units inside our stomach or in your intestine, helping you to digest alcohol" and something that would have broad medical benefits—beyond helping underage drinkers hide their partying from parents.

163

a more old-fashioned option as effective at reducing hangover symptoms: the hair of the dog that bit you. Drinking a small amount of alcohol (no more than one mimosa or Bloody Mary) after waking up with a headache or nausea has been found to significantly reduce the symptoms. This is because those suffering from hangovers are actually reacting to a small amount of methanol, which an alcoholic drink displaces with ethanol, relieving discomfort—at least temporarily.

164

Beer is a great workout recovery drink. In a study comparing it to water and energy drinks, beer was actually found to provide the speediest rehydration, in addition to offering sugars and potassium that help the transport of essential enzymes and nutrients through the body. That's not to say you should binge drink after a run: the scientists found that beer's benefits dropped off after twelve ounces.

165

Orange juice does not help cure a cold. While daily supplements of vitamin C have been found to slightly reduce the frequency and duration of a cold, once you start feeling sniffly, even very high dosages of the stuff will have no impact. Decades of studies have found that once symptoms appear, you can drink gallons of orange juice, but that cold is not going to get any better than if you were drinking water—or beer, for that matter.

166

Breakfast is not actually the most important meal of the day. True, some studies have associated eating breakfast with weight loss and lower risk of coronary heart disease. But in fact, a meta-analysis of these studies found only a correlation—not causation—between the two, and that many of these studies were funded by the food industry itself, which has obvious motives for encouraging people to have three square meals a day (or more). As the *New York Times* concluded upon reviewing all findings, only one deduction about breakfast could be made: "If you're hungry, eat."

167

In 1966, the folks at Quaker Oats Company decided that shoppers were tired of eating their cereal with a spoon, so they introduced Cap'n Crunch Ship Shake liquid cereal. The powdered breakfast drink, made of oat flour, could be mixed with milk to create Cap'n Crunch you could drink. It came in butterscotch, chocolate, and chocolate malt flavors—along with a special plastic mug in which to shake and drink it. On one package, the Cap'n himself told shoppers: "Ship Shake is so good, I not only drink it at breakfast, I have it at bedtime too!"

168

In the 1970s, McDonald's attempted to break into the breakfast cereal market with McCrunch: lightly sweetened cereal in the shape of the brand's famous arches, which came in chocolate, strawberry, and vanilla flavors (with a popular Happy Meal toy in each box, of course). After the success of the Egg McMuffin, launched in 1972, the company sought to expand further into the breakfast market. They were wrong. Despite an aggressive ad campaign featuring Ronald McDonald himself, the cereal never caught on with diners.

169

Kentucky Fried Chicken changed its name to KFC in 1990 because the word "fried" had become synonymous with "unhealthy." Rumors persist to this day that the name change came as a result of the Food and Drug Administration instructing the company that it could no longer advertise the hormone-filled, "mutant" chicken meat it sold as "chicken." But the real reason was because a newly health-oriented America had become more sensitive to phrases like "high cholesterol," "fattening," and "fried." The Colonel had to clean up his image, and the name change proved a simple solution.

170

*S*trawberry Frappuccinos used to contain bits of thousands of tiny bugs. Until 2012, the red dye that Starbucks used in its creamy drink was sourced from insect farms in South and Central America. Farmers there attract tiny cochineal insects with cactus leaves, where the bugs burrow and nest until harvest time, when farmers scrape them off by the tens of thousands, crushing them and drying them to produce a deep red dye (about seventy thousand insects create one pound of dye). An outcry from customers who preferred not to eat bug parts led Starbucks to switch to a different red ingredient in 2012, but the dye continues to be used in everything from Nerds candy to lipstick.

171

Mascara provides another example of an unlikely makeup ingredient: several top-selling brands contain bat guano. The dung of the cave-dwelling creatures, dried into a crystalline form, serves as a nutrient-rich element that works as a natural thickener. Though it has grown less popular across the cosmetics industry, it continues to be used by a number of top mascara brands (which we won't name here). So double-check the label if you're squeamish about guano on your lashes.

172

Eating bugs has enormous health benefits. Crickets and cockroaches are packed with B^{12} vitamins, ants and caterpillars are full of calcium, and aquatic insects come equipped with essential fatty acids that put salmon and sardines to shame. Dried grasshoppers are low in fat and high in protein (about 60 percent protein, 11 percent carbohydrate, and 2 percent fat) and pack more calories per pound than beef (one test put a pound of hoppers at 1,365 calories per pound compared to 1,240 calories of cooked medium-fat beef). Even better: insects require a fraction of the water and nourishment that livestock requires, making bugs one of the most efficient, inexpensive (and, depending on how they are prepared, delicious) sources of nourishment. Now, if only we could make them look a little more appetizing.

173

Nutmeg can make you hallucinate. The spice, often sprinkled on top of eggnog or apple pie, contains myristicin, which can impact the way the brain works if taken in large doses, creating a hallucinogenic buzz that can last as long as two days. The likely reason it hasn't become a more popular drug is the unpleasant side effects it causes, including nausea and vomiting (coincidentally, the same side effects of drinking too much eggnog).

174

The chocolate bars Milky Way and 3 Musketeers were switched at birth. Both released the same day in a limited run in the Minneapolis area (where Mars, Inc., was headquartered), an error was made in the labeling. What was supposed to be a "3 Musketeers"—the bar with the three ingredients of caramel, nougat, and a chocolate coating—erroneously became "Milky Way," and the creamy chocolate nougat bar meant to be "Milky Way" accidentally earned the name "3 Musketeers." While the executives in the product development department were furious, the enthusiastic response the incorrectly named bars received led the company president to order that the bars remain switched.

175

The United States loves its ice cream, but in fact it is only the third-highest consumer of the stuff: We are consistently out-eaten by both Australia and New Zealand. According to Euromonitor International, for at least five years running Australia has consumed the most ice cream (17.9L per capita in 2010), New Zealand the second most (with 15.8L per capita), followed by the U.S., with just 14.2L per capita. Perhaps even more sad for those who think of ice cream as an especially American dish: the dessert was not invented in the United States. Italian scientists get credit for discovering that mixing salt with ice caused it to become naturally colder—allowing for the freezing of cream desserts. However, while Italians may have invented it, Americans are the ones who popularized it.

176

*Y*ou *should* be wary of singing "Happy Birthday to You." Composed by American sisters Patty and Mildred Hill in the late nineteenth century (then known as "Good Morning to All"), it has since been dubbed "the most recognized song in the English language." But beware performing it: Warner Music Group, which owns the rights to the lyrics, has claimed copyright for every use of the song in any film, television show, or public performance (where most of those in attendance are not friends or family). And they collect a tidy $2 million annually from insurers on permission fees to use it—even as lawyers point out that "due to a lack of evidence about who wrote the words; defective copyright notice; and a failure to file a proper renewal application," they don't really have a claim on it anymore.

177

$\mathcal{T}$*he Hokey* Pokey might be hate speech. The song and dance, a staple at children's parties and family reunions going back decades, originated as a parody of Catholicism. The name derives from "hocus pocus," a mocking version of the Latin phrase *Hoc corpus meum* ("This is my body") said by the priest during Mass, while the silly dance is an imitation of the movements he performs. The controversy led to the song and dance being banned for a period at all sporting events throughout the United Kingdom.

178

It's very unlikely Marie Antoinette ever said, "let them eat cake." While legend has it that she said the phrase upon learning that the people of France were starving due to a bread shortage, no famines actually occurred during the reign of her husband, Louis XVI. The phrase was first noted by Jean-Jacques Rousseau in his autobiography, where he attributed them only to a "great princess." At the time he wrote of it, Antoinette would have been just fourteen years old and living in Austria (she didn't move to France until a year after Rousseau finished the book), making it unlikely she was the princess to whom he referred.

179

Paul Revere never shouted, "The British are coming!" His operation of alerting the colonial militia of the approach of British forces depended on secrecy: many English troops were hiding in the Massachusetts countryside, and plenty of colonists considered themselves more loyal to the Crown than the colonies. Shouting about the Red Coats' arrival would have alerted the enemy unnecessarily. Instead, he told trusted patriots along his route of what he had seen, quietly and surreptitiously.

180

Martin Luther King, Jr., improvised the most famous part of his "I Have a Dream" speech. King had written the speech in longhand the night before, on August 27, 1963, and the written version did not include the phrase "I have a dream." When he took to the podium before one-quarter million people in front of the Lincoln Memorial in Washington, D.C., much of what he delivered stuck to the script. That changed as he reached the end of his prepared remarks, and singer Mahalia Jackson, on stage nearby, shouted to him, "Tell them about the dream, Martin!" referring to a refrain he had used in recent sermons. King looked at the crowd and, as he would later describe, "all of a sudden this thing came to me that I have used—I'd used it many times before, that thing about 'I have a dream'— and I just felt that I wanted to use it here." His instincts proved just right.

181

Rosa Parks was not sitting in the "whites only" section of the bus when she was arrested. Municipal buses in Montgomery, Alabama, had thirty-six seats, and only the first ten were designated for whites, with the middle sixteen as first-come-first-serve (though the bus driver would rearrange seats to give whites priority). Parks was sitting in the front row of this middle section, next to several other black people. As the bus filled, all those in the middle section were asked to move to the back and make way for white passengers. All but Parks obliged, and the rest is history.

182

Rosa Parks' refusal to give up her seat was historic not only because she was black, but because she was a woman. While there had been black men who had refused and been physically removed, Parks was the first black woman to do so. It proved more galvanizing to civil rights activists and the African-American community to see a woman arrested, and it helped the event become the catalyst that sparked the Montgomery bus boycott.

183

Women's fight for the vote is well known, but they also had to fight for the right to smoke in public. The Women's Christian Temperance Union put most of its energy toward getting alcohol prohibited, but it also campaigned against women smoking in public. That did not go over well with the women of New York, who in 1929 went so far as to hold a "Torches of Freedom" march promoting women's right to smoke in public. Dressing as suffragettes, about a dozen women marched in the annual Easter Parade down Fifth Avenue, smoking cigarettes and carrying placards declaring cigarettes "torches of liberty."

184

Joan of Arc is honored as a hero in France and a saint in the Catholic Church, but she also was a pioneer in the field of hairstyling. The voices she heard as a teenager telling her to eject the English from France also urged her to don men's clothing and cut her hair short (a useful style in battle, if nothing else). When Antoine de Paris, a celebrated Parisian hairstylist during the early twentieth century (and the world's first celebrity hairdresser), introduced a new, short "bob" style on his clients, he pointed to Joan of Arc as his inspiration. The style soon exploded in popularity and became a signature of the Jazz Age, thanks to the unlikely source.

185

*D*espite the common assumption, women convicted during the Salem witch trials were never burned at the stake. In fact, they were most often hung. When a pair of girls began having fits in the spring of 1692 in Salem Village, Massachusetts, it set off a wave of witch-hunting mania that led to the convictions and execution of twenty people. The trials were travesties of justice, and the treatment of the convicted was cruel (with several people dying in prison), and their punishment severe. But at no point did it include burning at the stake—a practice that had by then been banned in England, and therefore its colonies.

186

In sixteenth- and seventeenth-century Britain, women who spoke in a way that was considered inappropriate could be put in "branks," a nasty muzzle that locked around her head and on some occasions came with a spiked plate that would be inserted into the wearer's mouth to prevent the tongue from moving. Also called the "scold's bridle" or "witch's bridle," it was often used to humiliate women who had transgressed in some way, and in some cases would make things even less pleasant for the wearer by attaching it to a town tollbooth or cross.

187

arguably worse when it comes to torture wear were "Judas Shoes." These metal boxes with small spikes on the bottom (and in some cases the sides) would be strapped to the feet of criminals in sixteenth-century Scotland. The wearers were forced to march through town—propelled by a flogging or an angry mob—taking one agonizing step after another as the spikes pierced their feet repeatedly. Some were forced to walk for hours in this way and could not stop until they actually passed out from loss of blood.

188

The buckle worn on the brim of Puritan hats was meant—like so many other behaviors of this righteous crowd—to ward off the devil. The stylish detail, added to the conical hats, or *capotains*, worn by Puritan men in the middle of the sixteenth century, grew out of sermons that urged the virtuous to "fortify yourself against sin." Soon men in the Connecticut Colony began to don the buckles as a way to show they were heeding the advice.

189

For centuries, Europeans hid shoes in chimneys, under floors, and in the roofs of buildings in order to ward off evil spirits or bring good luck to their home. Shoes have been found in these nooks of homes dating as far back as the early sixteenth century. So many have been found that the Northampton Museums and Art Gallery in the United Kingdom has created a "concealed shoe index" to track these discoveries, noting details about the footwear, the building in which it was found, and the location. So far, it has tracked about 1,900 concealed shoes, many of which are from children and almost all without the other half of the pair.

190

The fashion "rule" against wearing white after Labor Day originated from a Puritan law. In the 1660s, female colonists in Massachusetts began wearing white satin, which was all the rage in Europe at the time. The strict Puritan men demanded they stop wearing the fabric, which they believed to be coquettish and offensive to God, as well as too European. But the style proved resilient and many women continued wearing satin. Eventually a compromise was struck: white could be worn in summer, but no later.

191

*T*he *high* heels of today pale in comparison to what elite Venetian women wore in the sixteenth and seventeenth centuries. The *chopine*, similar to clogs and placed over one's shoe, could rise higher than a foot and a half. This served not just to draw attention to the wearer, but allowed her to keep her shoes and dress from being soiled by the mud (and even more disgusting substances) that filled Europe's streets. Shakespeare captured another appeal of the footwear in a line from *Hamlet*: "Your ladyship is nearer to heaven than when I saw you last, by the altitude of a chopine."

192

Watches in print ads and billboards are almost always set at 10:10. Some theorize that advertisers began doing this with the very first print ads. Others claim that the tradition began as a way to commemorate the exact time when President Abraham Lincoln was shot. While Lincoln was shot at about that time (historians put it closer to 10:13 in the evening), the actual reason is much more mundane: by having the hour hand on ten and the minute hand on two, it leaves plenty of room to show off the name of the watch brand (which typically appears under the twelve).

193

Those who feel Morgan Freeman and Harrison Ford look a bit ridiculous wearing an earring might consider another older guy who decorated his earlobe: William Shakespeare. The beloved playwright was consistently depicted in seventeenth-century portraits wearing a single shiny gold hoop earring from his left ear. With his receding hairline, loose shirts, and well-trimmed beard, the Bard was pioneering the "aging rock star" look in the Renaissance.

194

a **Florida cruise** service was shut down in 1993 when it was exposed that it provided a "bonus service" to interested passengers: assisted suicide. The independent cruise service Gold Horizon Line had operated for decades, providing tours of the Caribbean to a customer base consisting mainly of Florida-based retirees. As it ran into financial troubles, the cruise line expanded its services with the "off-menu" option of euthanasia. For a little more than $10,000, a passenger and his or her partner could take a weeklong cruise, which concluded (in international waters, where such things are harder to prosecute) with the onboard doctor helping speed them on their way. The *Gold Horizon*'s operator was convicted only of fraud, since it turned out no customers took him up on the special offer.

195

A penny costs 1.7 cents to produce. According to the U.S. Government Accountability Office, the U.S. Mint spends an average of 1.7 cents to create each one-cent coin. Not only that, a nickel costs eight cents to produce. For years, the government has discussed ways to reduce the expense, from using different metal to getting rid of the denominations altogether, but they've faced pushback from vending machine companies, among others, that protest that modifying their coin machines could cost as much as $10 billion. For now, it looks like we're stuck with pricey pennies.

196

That $20 bill in your pocket may contain bits of $1, $5, and $100 bills. Every year, the Federal Reserve removes from circulation and shreds more than five thousand tons of paper currency. Those destroyed bills are then pulped and recycled to help manufacture new bills. About 10 percent of every new bill is made from old ones, partly as a cost-saving measure (the materials to make currency aren't cheap). So look closely at that dollar in your pocket—it might contain more value than at first appears.

197

Piggy banks used to actually be made from pigs. The term grew out of a practice by gentlemen in medieval England who stored their coins in satchels made from dried pigskin. Each sack, about three inches long and two inches wide, became known as a "pig pouch" and later would be called a "pig bank." As pockets became widespread (see fact 8) and men left their valuables at home, usually in small chests or ceramic pots, the name continued to be used. By the nineteenth century, manufacturers were creating "piggy banks" that actually looked like pigs.

198

a small number of U.S. bills include a star after the serial number. Known as a "tracking star," this symbol was once used by the government to follow a sample of all the bills it produced. Banks were required to report whenever they received one of the tracked bills, which helped the federal government monitor how currency was circulating. The practice ceased to be necessary as banking technology evolved, but the stars continue to be used.

199

Cleopatra was probably not Egyptian. The woman whom more than any other figure (outside of King Tut) we associate with Ancient Egypt was actually Greek, a descendent of Ptolemy, a trusted Macedonian general of Alexander the Great. The Ptolemaic Dynasty ruled Egypt for about three hundred years and during that time maintained their Greek culture in many ways. Cleopatra embraced her adopted country more than other in her family, learning to speak Egyptian while few others in the dynasty had bothered.

200

History is written by the winners—even when they were actually losers. In 1288 BC, Egyptian Pharaoh Ramses II launched an attack on the neighboring Hittite Empire. They failed to capture the main city of Kadesh and had to retreat to Egypt. As Egyptologist John A. Wilson wrote, "[Ramses II] was badly taken by surprise in that battle and returned to Egypt without achieving his objectives." But instead of accepting defeat, Ramses declared the battle had been a huge success for his side and documented his "victory" in scenes and texts throughout the region. For centuries, writers and historians took his version of events at face value—until more recently discovered documents and artifacts from the era revealed the real story of the events.

Score Cards

Write number correct for each column.
Determine score for each on next page.

1 *Skinny Jeans, Vaseline, and Frisbee*

CHAPTER I
1. F / AF
2. F / AF
3. F / AF
4. F / AF
5. F / AF
6. F / AF
7. F / AF
8. F / AF
9. F / AF
10. F / AF

11. F / AF
12. F / AF
13. F / AF
14. F / AF
15. F / AF
16. F / AF
17. F / AF
18. F / AF
19. F / AF
20. F / AF

For each entry, circle whether it is a **FACT** ("F") or **ALTERNATIVE FACT** ("AF").

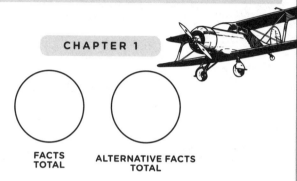

CHAPTER 1

( )

FACTS
TOTAL

( )

ALTERNATIVE FACTS
TOTAL

21. F / AF	
22. F / AF	
23. F / AF	
24. F / AF	
25. F / AF	
26. F / AF	
27. F / AF	
28. F / AF	
29. F / AF	
30. F / AF	

31. F / AF
32. F / AF
33. F / AF
34. F / AF
35. F / AF
36. F / AF
37. F / AF
38. F / AF
39. F / AF
40. F / AF

Score Cards

Write number correct for each column.
Determine score for each on next page.

2 Dracula, Bubonic Plague, and Knock-Knock Jokes

CHAPTER 2
41. F / AF
42. F / AF
43. F / AF
44. F / AF
45. F / AF
46. F / AF
47. F / AF
48. F / AF
49. F / AF

50. F / AF
51. F / AF
52. F / AF
53. F / AF
54. F / AF
55. F / AF
56. F / AF
57. F / AF
58. F / AF
59. F / AF

CHAPTER 2

FACTS
TOTAL

ALTERNATIVE FACTS
TOTAL

70.	F / AF
71.	F / AF
72.	F / AF
73.	F / AF
74.	F / AF
75.	F / AF
76.	F / AF
77.	F / AF
78.	F / AF
79.	F / AF
80.	F / AF

60.	F / AF
61.	F / AF
62.	F / AF
63.	F / AF
64.	F / AF
65.	F / AF
66.	F / AF
67.	F / AF
68.	F / AF
69.	F / AF

Score Cards

Write number correct for each column.
Determine score for each on next page.

3 *Jet Lag, Jellyfish, and Cricket Ears*

CHAPTER 3
81. F / AF
82. F / AF
83. F / AF
84. F / AF
85. F / AF
86. F / AF
87. F / AF
88. F / AF
89. F / AF

90. F / AF
91. F / AF
92. F / AF
93. F / AF
94. F / AF
95. F / AF
96. F / AF
97. F / AF
98. F / AF
99. F / AF

CHAPTER 3

FACTS
TOTAL

ALTERNATIVE FACTS
TOTAL

100. F / AF	**110.** F / AF
101. F / AF	**111.** F / AF
102. F / AF	**112.** F / AF
103. F / AF	**113.** F / AF
104. F / AF	**114.** F / AF
105. F / AF	**115.** F / AF
106. F / AF	**116.** F / AF
107. F / AF	**117.** F / AF
108. F / AF	**118.** F / AF
109. F / AF	**119.** F / AF

Score Cards

Write number correct for each column.
Determine score for each on next page.

Outhouses, Oreos, and Niagara Falls

CHAPTER 4
120. F / AF
121. F / AF
122. F / AF
123. F / AF
124. F / AF
125. F / AF
126. F / AF
127. F / AF
128. F / AF
129. F / AF

130. F / AF
131. F / AF
132. F / AF
133. F / AF
134. F / AF
135. F / AF
136. F / AF
137. F / AF
138. F / AF
139. F / AF

CHAPTER 4

FACTS
TOTAL

ALTERNATIVE FACTS
TOTAL

140.	F / AF
141.	F / AF
142.	F / AF
143.	F / AF
144.	F / AF
145.	F / AF
146.	F / AF
147.	F / AF
148.	F / AF
149.	F / AF

150.	F / AF
151.	F / AF
152.	F / AF
153.	F / AF
154.	F / AF
155.	F / AF
156.	F / AF
157.	F / AF
158.	F / AF
159.	F / AF
160.	F / AF

Score Cards

Write number correct for each column.
Determine score for each on next page.

5 **High Heels, Hokey Pokey, and Piggy Banks**

CHAPTER 5
161. F / AF
162. F / AF
163. F / AF
164. F / AF
165. F / AF
166. F / AF
167. F / AF
168. F / AF
169. F / AF

170. F / AF
171. F / AF
172. F / AF
173. F / AF
174. F / AF
175. F / AF
176. F / AF
177. F / AF
178. F / AF
179. F / AF

CHAPTER 5

○ ○

FACTS
TOTAL

ALTERNATIVE FACTS
TOTAL

190.	F / AF
191.	F / AF
192.	F / AF
193.	F / AF
194.	F / AF
195.	F / AF
196.	F / AF
197.	F / AF
198.	F / AF
199.	F / AF
200.	F / AF

180.	F / AF
181.	F / AF
182.	F / AF
183.	F / AF
184.	F / AF
185.	F / AF
186.	F / AF
187.	F / AF
188.	F / AF
189.	F / AF

Score

Write the total number correct for each chapter. Determine score for each below.

CHAPTER 1

CHAPTER 2

CHAPTER 3

CHAPTER 4   **CHAPTER 5**

35–40 CORRECT: *You know* the capital of every country and are basically a genius knower of facts.

25–34 CORRECT: *You know* that 100 percent of statistics are made up half the time.

15–24 CORRECT: Strong *but* you could be better.

11–14 CORRECT: *A bit slow,* but hang in there.

6–10 CORRECT: *Read a few* more books.

0–5 CORRECT: *Stop getting* the news from your garden gnome.

Answer Key

1. **FACT.** "You'll Go Blind: Does Watching Television Close-Up Really Harm Eyesight?" *Scientific American*, accessed April 25, 2017, https://www.scientificamerican.com/article/earth-talk-tv-eyesight/.

2. **FACT.** William E. Morgan, DC, "Skinny Jeans Syndrome," accessed May 23, 2017, http://drmorgan.info/clinicians-corner/meralgia-paresthetica-skinny-jean-syndrome/.

3. **FACT.** Charles Panati, *Extraordinary Origins of Everyday Things* (New York: William Morrow, 1987).

4. **FACT.** "Charcoal Drawing – Study of Foliage," *Ingall's Home and Art Magazine, vol.* 4, (Lynn, Massachusetts: J.F. Ingalls, 1891), 250.

5. **ALTERNATIVE FACT.** Though Chesebrough did eat a spoonful of Vaseline a day, it was never marketed as something to be eaten.

6. **FACT.** "A Q-Tips Cotton Swabs History," accessed May 23, 2017, http://www.qtips.com/home/about.

7. **ALTERNATIVE FACT.** Several theories of this expression's origin exist (including that the eighty-sixth floor of the Empire State Building is the most popular for those looking to jump) but this is not one of them.

8. **FACT.** Charles Panati, *Extraordinary Origins of Everyday Things* (New York: William Morrow, 1987).

9. **ALTERNATIVE FACT.** The myth that Boleyn had an extra finger was introduced by Catholic propagandist Nicholas Sanders in a pamphlet written in 1586 claiming she also had "a projecting tooth" and large cyst under her chin. There is no evidence any of this was true.

10. **FACT.** Leslie Stephen, ed., *Dictionary of National Biography, vol. XVII, Edward–Erskine* (New York: Macmillan and Co., 1889), 230; Martin Andrew Sharp Hume, *The Courtships of Queen Elizabeth* (London: T. Fisher Unwin, 1896), 323.

11. **FACT.** History Extra, "7 things you (probably) didn't know about Elizabeth!," Tracy Borman, BBC, July 30, 2015, http://www.historyextra.com/article/facts-elizabethi.

12.   **FACT.** Jordan Almond, *Dictionary of Word Origins* (New York: Citadel Press, 1985), 220.

13.   **FACT.** "John Duns Scotus," *Stanford Encyclopedia of Philosophy*, accessed May 23, 2017, https://plato.stanford.edu/entries/duns-scotus/. Maurice Waite, ed., *Pocket Oxford English Dictionary*, 11th ed. (Oxford: Oxford University Press, 2013), 277.

14.   **ALTERNATIVE FACT.** The term actually originated in the 1930s, referring to a fly ball that barely makes it out of the infield.

15.   **ALTERNATIVE FACT.** Though Doubleday has been historically believed to have invented baseball, a 1953 investigation by Congress determined a New York firefighter named Alexander Joy Cartwright, Jr., to be the true inventor.

16.   **ALTERNATIVE FACT.** This is a popular myth about Castro but no evidence supports it. The Yankees did not start scouting in Cuba until the 1960s, after the revolution had occurred and Castro had risen to power. "No, Fidel Castro Wasn't Nearly A New York Yankee," *NPR*, November 30, 2016, http://www.npr.org/2016/11/30/503752196/no-fidel-castro-wasnt-nearly-a-new-york-yankee.

17.   **FACT.** Joshua Robinson, "Steelers Shared Resources With 2 Teams During World War II," *New York Times*, January 14, 2009, http://www.nytimes.com/2009/01/15/sports/football/15steagles.html.

18.   **ALTERNATIVE FACT.** Golf is a Dutch word dating back to the fifteenth century and was never an acronym.

19.   **ALTERNATIVE FACT.** Although Darrow claimed credit for Monopoly and made millions from it, the concept originated years earlier in 1903 with Elizabeth Magie, a progressive activist who designed "the Landlord's Game" as a protest against contemporary monopolists like Andrew Carnegie. Participants could play two ways: one where they won by creating wealth and the other by creating a monopoly. Darrow, using street names from a customized version created by an Atlantic City Quaker community, sold the pro-monopoly idea to Parker Brothers. Magie reportedly earned only $500 for the game.

20. **ALTERNATIVE FACT.** Some version of this urban legend has been floating around since the dolls were introduced, but it has no basis in reality. Roberts began making the dolls by hand in 1978, inspired by the quilts made by his mother.

21. **FACT.** Michael Liedtke, "How the Frisbee got its name," *New York Times*, June 17, 2007, http://www.nytimes.com/2007/06/17/business/worldbusiness/17iht-frisbee.1.6170947.html.

22. **ALTERNATIVE FACT.** The name was an invention by businesswoman Marjorie Husted, who sought an "all-American" name that would personalize the brand—though "Crocker" was used as a tribute to Washburn-Crosby Director William Crocker.

23. **FACT.** "No longer Famous, Wally Amos still baking," *Associated Press*, July 13, 2007, http://www.nbcnews.com/id/19731831/ns/business-us_business/t/no-longer-famous-wally-amos-still-baking/.

24. **FACT.** Olivier Darmon, *Michelin Man: 100 Years of Bibendum* (London: Conran Octopus, 1998).

25. **FACT.** "Was the Comic Strip 'Peanuts' Renamed 'Radishes' in Denmark?" *Snopes*, April 16, 2015, http://www.snopes.com/language/misxlate/peanuts.asp.

26. **ALTERNATIVE FACT.** Miyamoto himself explained that the word donkey was selected deliberately—to project a sense of stubbornness, with Kong connoting "gorilla." David Mikkelson, "Donkey Kong Naming," *Snopes*, July 11, 2014, http://www.snopes.com/business/misxlate/donkeykong.asp.

27. **FACT.** David McNamee, "Hey, what's that sound: the Katzenklavier," *The Guardian,* April 19, 2010, https://www.theguardian.com/music/2010/apr/19/katzenklavier-music-piano-cats.

28. **FACT.** "Did Nero really fiddle while Rome burned?" *History.com*, November 20, 2012, http://www.history.com/news/ask-history/did-nero-really-fiddle-while-rome-burned.

29. **ALTERNATIVE FACT.** The *Gjallarhorn* is a horn in Norse mythology blown by a god to bring about Ragnarok. The loudest instrument, according to *Guinness*, is a 33,000-pipe Baroque organ housed in Atlantic City's Boardwalk Hall Auditorium.

30. **FACT.** Christine Lund, "News," April 17, 2015, http://www.mobilephonethrowing.fi/news.

31. **FACT.** Federal Communications Commission, "Wireless Devices at Gas Stations," October 27, 2016, https://transition.fcc.gov/cgb/consumerfacts/wirelessgas.pdf.

32. **ALTERNATIVE FACT.** As *Consumer Reports* points out, gasoline is stored in underground tanks, so its temperature will remain unchanged no matter the weather. "Debunking fuel-economy myths," *Consumer Reports*, August 2012, http://www.consumerreports.org/cro/magazine/2012/08/debunking-fuel-economy-myths/index.htm.

33. **FACT.** Diana Kurylko, "Model T had many shades; black dried fastest," *Automotive News*, June 16, 2003, http://www.autonews.com/article/20030616/SUB/306160713/model-t-had-many-shades%3B-black-dried-fastest. Ken Jennings, "The Debunker: Did Model T Ford Only Come in Black?" December 10, 2013, https://www.woot.com/blog/post/the-debunker-did-the-model-t-ford-only-come-in-black.

34. **ALTERNATIVE FACT.** There was indeed a car graveyard in this part of Belgium, but despite the popular myth, they did not come from American soldiers—many of the cars were models from the 1960s and 1970s.

35. **FACT.** Charles Cruickshank, *German Occupation of the Channel Islands* (Oxford: Oxford University Press, 1975).

36. **ALTERNATIVE FACT.** Reagan was never seriously considered for the role, but a press release the studio issued early in *Casablanca*'s development names him, which has fueled the rumor ever since.

37. **ALTERNATIVE FACT.** They were never called "the Tracys," although Spencer Tracy did receive all those awards and nominations.

38. **FACT.** Kirthana Ramisetti, "10 surprising fun facts about the Oscars," *New York Daily News*, February 21, 2015, http://www.nydailynews.com/entertainment/movies/oscars-2015-10-fun-facts-hollywood-night-article-1.2123411.

39. **FACT.** Ernie Smith, "The Slow Demise of Asbestos, the Carcinogen that Gave 'The Wizard of Oz' Snow," *Atlas Obscura*, August 1, 2016, http://www.atlasobscura.com/articles/the-slow-demise-of-asbestos-the-carcinogen-that-gave-the-wizard-of-oz-snow.

40. **FACT.** David Mikkelson, "Jingle Bells: A Thanksgiving Carol," *Snopes*, December 18, 2014, http://www.snopes.com/holidays/christmas/music/jinglebells.asp.

41. **ALTERNATIVE FACT.** Coca-Cola is often erroneously given credit for inventing or modernizing the image of Santa, but their version was little different from the one that had been well known since the late 1800s, first popularized by cartoonist Thomas Nast.

42. **FACT.** Liam Stack, "Valentine's Day: Did It Start as a Roman Party or to Celebrate an Execution?" *New York Times*, February 14, 2017, https://www.nytimes.com/2017/02/14/style/valentines-day-facts-history.html?_r=0.

43. **FACT.** Olivia B. Waxman, "How Green Became Associated With St. Patrick's Day and All Things Irish," *TIME*, March 16, 2017, http://time.com/4699771/green-irish-st-patricks-day-color/. Shaylyn Esposito, "Should We Be Wearing Blue on St. Patrick's Day?" March 17, 2015, http://www.smithsonianmag.com/arts-culture/should-st-patricks-day-be-blue-180954572/.

44. **FACT.** Nicholas Rogers, *Halloween: From Pagan Ritual to Party Night* (Oxford: Oxford University Press, 2002), 57.

45. **ALTERNATIVE FACT.** Vlad was by all accounts a nasty guy in battle, but the connections to the Count end there. No evidence exists that he drank blood or had any other similarities to Stoker's invention.

46. **FACT.** Ann Mah, "Where Dracula Was Born, and It's Not Transylvania," *New York Times,* September 8, 2015, https://www.nytimes.com/2015/09/13/travel/bram-stoker-dracula-yorkshire.html. Shaun Turton, "In the Blood," *Slate*, August 29, 2014, http://www.slate.com/articles/news_and_politics/roads/2014/08/bram_stoker_s_great_grandnephew_wants_to_attract_visitors_to_the_remote.html.

47. **ALTERNATIVE FACT.** Dickens is often falsely believed to have been paid by the word. While his novels' lengths were often dictated in advance, his earnings were pegged to the number of books he sold, not the number of words.

48. **FACT.** "James Joyce Dies; Wrote 'Ulysses,'" *New York Times*, January 13, 1941, http://www.nytimes.com/learning/general/onthisday/bday/0202.html. Peter Spielberg, James Joyce's Manuscripts & Letters at the University of Buffalo (Buffalo, NY: University of Buffalo, 1962).

49. **ALTERNATIVE FACT.** Though Hemingway was a serious drinker, he stayed sober while he wrote. When asked if it were true that he took a pitcher of martinis to work each morning, he replied, "Jeezus Christ! Have you ever heard of anyone who drank while he worked? You're thinking of Faulkner."

50. **FACT.** Hellen Kiloran, *The Critical Reception of Edith Wharton* (Rochester: Camden House, 2001), 80.

51. **ALTERNATIVE FACT.** The phrase originated as the name of a comic strip that launched in 1913, but some historians believe the phrase referred to Wharton's family on the side of her prestigious father, George Frederic Jones.

52. **FACT.** Laura C. Lambdin and Robert T. Lambdin, eds., "Thomas Stearns Eliot," *Arthurian Writers: A Biographical Encyclopedia* (Westport, Connecticut: Greenwood Press, 2008), 246.

53. **ALTERNATIVE FACT.** Knock-knock jokes did not become widespread until the twentieth century. They were likely popularized by vice presidential candidate Colonel Frank Knox, who made the jokes a staple of his widely covered campaign stops throughout 1936. Once the door was opened to them, it could never be shut. Linton Weeks, "The Secret History of Knock-Knock Jokes," *NPR*, March 3, 2015, http://www.npr.org/sections/npr-history-dept/2015/03/03/389865887/the-secret-history-of-knock-knock-jokes.

54. **ALTERNATIVE FACT.** Actually, both theories are wrong. Though the origin of the expression remains unclear, it appears in newspapers as far back as the 1910s—long predating concrete mixers or World War II ammunition belts. Bonus fact: the expression was originally "the whole six yards." Jennifer Schuessler, "The Whole Nine Yards About a Phrase's Origin," *New York Times*, December 26, 2012, http://www.nytimes.com/2012/12/27/books/the-whole-nine-yards-seeking-a-phrases-origin.html.

55. **FACT.** Rachel Nuwer, "The First Use of OMG Was in a 1917 Letter to Winston Churchill," *Smithsonianmag.com*, November 27, 2012, http://www.smithsonianmag.com/smart-news/the-first-use-of-omg-was-in-a-1917-letter-to-winston-churchill-145636383/.

56. **FACT.** Barbara Mikkelson, "Etymology of Blackmail," *Snopes*, April 10, 2014, http://www.snopes.com/language/colors/blackmail.asp.

57. **ALTERNATIVE FACT.** While medieval tunnels (called erdstalls) have been found scattered throughout Europe, they don't form a connected passageway.

58. **FACT.** Brenda Fowler, *Iceman* (Chicago: The University of Chicago Press, 2000), 205.

59. **ALTERNATIVE FACT.** "Cloud nine" did not come into common use until the 1950s, as a catch phrase on the radio show Johnny Dollar. While it's origin is unclear, the phrase "cloud seven" was used as early as the late nineteenth century, likely a riff on the expression "seventh heaven." Michael Quinion, *Why is Q Always Followed by U?* (New York: Particular Books, 2009).

60. **FACT.** Jeffrey Burton Russell, *Inventing the Flat Earth: Columbus and Modern Historians* (New York: Praeger, 1991), 3.

61. **ALTERNATIVE FACT.** In fact, the plague hit the wealthy almost as hard as the poor. Accounts of the period record that well-funded friaries and monasteries, knights, ladies, and merchants were rocked by the plague. "Plague and economics," *The Economist*, December 23, 1999, http://www.economist.com/node/346790.

62. **ALTERNATIVE FACT.** Weill Cornell did initially say they found evidence of the bubonic plague, but quickly walked back the claim (and never said anything about E. coli or gonorrhea), and New York City's health department stated, "We don't know what bacteria they found, but it's definitely not the plague." Still, washing your hands is a good idea. Anemona Hartocollis, "Bubonic Plague in the Subway System? Don't Worry About It," *New York Times*, February 6, 2015, https://www.nytimes.com/2015/02/07/nyregion/bubonic-plague-in-the-subway-system-dont-worry-about-it.html.

63. **FACT.** Anthony Lambert, *Lambert's Railway Miscellany* (New York: Ebury Press, 2010), 73.

64. **FACT.** Jon Ostrower, "Why airplanes still have ashtrays. No, you can't smoke," *CNN Money*, March 9, 2017, http://money.cnn.com/2017/03/09/news/airplane-ashtrays/.

65. **FACT.** Amelia Earhart, *Last Flight* (New York: Harcourt, Brace and Company, 1937).

66. **FACT.** "Railroads create the first time zones," *History.com*, accessed May 25, 2017, http://www.history.com/this-day-in-history/railroads-create-the-first-time-zones.

67. **FACT.** Henry Louis Gates, Jr., "Who Really Ran the Underground Railroad?" *The Root*, March 25, 2013, http://www.theroot.com/who-really-ran-the-underground-railroad-1790895697.

68. **ALTERNATIVE FACT.** This is a popular myth of the Underground Railroad, with no basis in fact. As Henry Louis Gates, Jr., explains, "Freedom quilts? Simply put, this is one of the oddest myths propagated in all of African-American history. If a slave family had the wherewithal to make a quilt, they used it to protect themselves against the cold." Henry Louis Gates, Jr., "Who Really Ran the Underground Railroad?" *The Root*, March 25, 2013, http://www.theroot.com/who-really-ran-the-underground-railroad-1790895697.

69. **FACT.** Kristen T. Oertel, *Harriet Tubman: Slavery, the Civil War, and Civil Rights in the 19th Century* (New York: Routledge Historical Americans, 2015).

70. **ALTERNATIVE FACT.** Despite the image in movies of Civil War soldiers swigging spirits and biting bullets to push through painful surgery, both chloroform and ether were widely available at this time, and more than 90 percent of surgeries made use of them. Laura Cutter, Tim Clarke, Jr., "Anesthesia Advances During the Civil War," *Military Medicine*, vol. 179, 1503, December 2014.

71. **FACT.** "Soothing Syrups," *New York Times*, August 30, 1910.

72. **ALTERNATIVE FACT.** There no documented case of such a "cosmetic hand transplant."

73. **ALTERNATIVE FACT.** Eyes do grow as we age—they are roughly two-thirds of their adult size at birth.

74.   **FACT.** David Zhang, Zhi Liu, Jing-qi Yan, Peng-fei Shi, "Tongue-Print: A Novel Biometrics Pattern," in Lee SW., Li S.Z., eds., *Advances in Biometrics* (ICB 2007, Lecture Notes in Computer Science, vol. 4642, Springer: Berlin Heidelberg, Germany).

75.   **ALTERNATIVE FACT.** Neither hair nor fingernails grows after death, though the skin around both retracts as it becomes dehydrated, making them appear longer.

76.   **ALTERNATIVE FACT.** Though cracking knuckles is caused by releasing gas from synovial fluid, there is no evidence that this contributes to arthritis (though some studies have found that it can reduce grip strength).

77.   **FACT.** Jason G. Goldman, "The myth of being 'double jointed,'" *BBC*, June 2, 2015, http://www.bbc.com/future/story/20150602-why-only-some-of-us-are-double-jointed.

78.   **FACT.** Robynne Boyd, "Do People Only Use 10 Percent of Their Brains?" *Scientific American*, February 7, 2008, https://www.scientificamerican.com/article/do-people-only-use-10-percent-of-their-brains/.

79.   **FACT.** "5 Other Disastrous Accidents Related to Sleep Deprivation," *Huffington Post,* December 3, 2013, http://www.huffingtonpost.com/2013/12/03/sleep-deprivation-accidents-disasters_n_4380349.html; Maanvi Singh, "Short on Sleep? You Could Be a Disaster Waiting to Happen," *NPR,* May 12, 2015, http://www.npr.org/sections/health-shots/2015/05/12/406137352/short-on-sleep-you-could-be-a-disaster-waiting-to-happen.

80.   **FACT.** Kevin McCue, "Thanksgiving, Turkey, and Tryptophan," American Chemical Society, November 22, 2004.

81.   **ALTERNATIVE FACT.** A daytime flight is actually better for fighting jet lag—that way when you land you can eat dinner and go to bed, helping to "resynchronize." More than drowsiness, alcohol causes dehydration—which compounds symptoms of jet lag. Drink water instead. Melissa Locker, "The Truth Behind Common Jet Lag Myths," *Travel + Leisure*, February 5, 2017, http://www.travelandleisure.com/airlines-airports/common-jet-lag-myths.

82. **ALTERNATIVE FACT.** While studies of brain activity have found pockets of neural activity in certain regions (for example, with speech emanating from the left side of the brain for right-handed people), on average, people use both sides of their brain equally. Christopher Wanjek, "Left Brain vs. Right: It's a Myth, Research Finds," *LiveScience*, September 3, 2013, http://www.livescience.com/39373-left-brain-right-brain-myth.html.

83. **ALTERNATIVE FACT.** There is no significant difference in hair width or coarseness after it is shaved. The hairs just feel stubbly when it regrows after shaving.

84. **FACT.** Rita Rubin, "40 chews per bite may be key to weight loss," *NBC News*, August 10, 2011. Walter Gratzer, *Terrors of the Table: The Curious History of Nutrition* (Oxford: Oxford University Press, 2005), 202.

85. **ALTERNATIVE FACT.** While images of vintage ads promoting tapeworm diet pills have surfaced online and sexist rumors circulate every few decades about high-profile women engaging in this bizarre fad diet, there is little evidence such pills ever existed or were popular.

86. **ALTERNATIVE FACT.** Higher levels of heat escape through your head because that's usually the part that's not covered with clothing. Researchers have found no evidence that your head releases more heat on average than other parts of the body exposed to the same conditions.

87. **FACT.** Jessica Cerretani, "Extra Sensory Perceptions," Harvard Medical School, https://hms.harvard.edu/news/harvard-medicine/extra-sensory-perceptions.

88. **FACT.** Mary Bagley, "Matter: Definition and the Five States of Matter," *LiveScience*, April 11, 2016, http://www.livescience.com/46506-states-of-matter.html.

89. **FACT.** Dan Nosowitz, "Which Animal Has the Most Extreme Sense of Hearing?" *Popular Science*, May 8, 2013, http://www.popsci.com/science/article/2013-05/which-animal-has-most-extreme-sense-hearing.

90. **FACT.** Ed Yong, "The insect that hears like a human, with ears on its knees," *Discover*, November 15, 2012.

91. **ALTERNATIVE FACT.** Contrary to the "blind as a bat" expression, bats actually can see, and sometimes when foraging they don't use echolocation at all, just their eyes.

92. **FACT.** Irving Wallace, David Wallechinsky, Amy Wallace, *Significa* (New York: E.P. Dutton, 1983), 11.

93. **ALTERNATIVE FACT.** This is a common myth of venomous snakes with no basis in reality. While baby snakes are a bit sloppy with their venom control, their venom glands are actually much smaller than adults' (for example, baby rattlesnakes deliver up to seventy milligrams of venom, while an adult can deliver more than six hundred milligrams).

94. **FACT.** Katie Zezima, "Death Does Not Deter Jellyfish Sting," *New York Times*, July 22, 2010, http://www.nytimes.com/2010/07/23/us/23jelly.html.

95. **FACT.** Mark Leyner and Billy Goldberg, *Why Do Men Have Nipples?* (New York: Three Rivers Press, 2005), 109.

96. **ALTERNATIVE FACT.** The hump is just a mound of fat and doesn't store water. But camels can go without hydration for seven days —mostly due to oval-shaped red blood cells which allow them to drink and retain large volumes of water. Jonathan Kingdon, *East African Mammals, Volume III Part B* (Chicago: The University of Chicago Press, 1979), 286.

97. **FACT.** Rachel Becker, "When Single Male Rodents Settle Down, They're Changed Forever," *National Geographic*, September 5, 2012, http://news.nationalgeographic.com/2015/09/150903-prairie-voles-sex-love-animals-science/.

98. **FACT.** "Ostrich: *Struthio camelus*," San Diego Zoo, http://animals.sandiegozoo.org/animals/ostrich.

99. **FACT.** George B. Schaller, *The Serengeti Lion: A Study of Predator-Prey Relations* (Chicago; University of Chicago Press, 1972), 254.

100. **ALTERNATIVE FACT.** This popular misconception was disproven by a research team that monitored a group of giraffes for more than 150 nights, which found they slept for an average of 4.6 hours a day.

101. **FACT.** Vidal Haddad Jr. and Ivan Sazima, "Piranha attacks on humans in southeast Brazil: epidemiology, natural history, and clinical treatment, with description of a bite outbreak," *Wilderness & Environmental Medicine,* Winter 2003, 249-54.

102. **FACT.** "Alligators in the White House Bathtub, Oh My!," Presidential Pet Museum, September 5, 2013, http://www.presidentialpetmuseum.com/blog/alligators-in-the-white-house/.

103. **ALTERNATIVE FACT.** Taft actually kept White House cows: Mooley Wooly was the first, followed by the more famous Pauline Wayne, a Holstein cow that grazed on the White House lawn and whose milk was enjoyed by the Tafts.

104. **ALTERNATIVE FACT.** Though it is made of Aquia Creek sandstone, and was partially burned during the War of 1812, the building has been white since its completion.

105. **FACT.** Rebecca Rupp, "Thomas Jefferson: President, Scholar, First Foodie," *National Geographic*, April 13, 2016, http://theplate. nationalgeographic.com/2016/04/13/thomas-jefferson-president-scholar-first-foodie/; Jack Mclaughlin, *Jefferson and Monticello: The Biography of a Builder* (New York: Henry Holt and Company, 1988), 229.

106. **FACT.** Ed Crews, "Drinking in Colonial America," *Colonial Williamsburg Journal*, Holiday 2007.

107. **ALTERNATIVE FACT.** Jefferson was in Paris at the time of the Constitution's signing, so he did not sign it at all.

108. **FACT.** National Constitution Center Staff, "Eight biggest Founding Father myths for National History Day," *Constitution Daily*, March 19, 2015, https://constitutioncenter.org/blog/eight-biggest-founding-fathers-myths-for-national-history-day/.

109. **ALTERNATIVE FACT.** There were several official versions of the Pledge of Allegiance—it did not originally have "of the United States of America" or "under God," but none included the word happiness. "The Pledge of Allegiance, http://www.ushistory.org/documents/pledge.htm.

110. **FACT.** "Fifteen Stars and Stripes," https://publications.usa.gov/epublications/ourflag/history4.htm.

111. **FACT.** Owen Edwards, "Abraham Lincoln Is the Only President Ever to Have a Patent," *Smithsonian Magazine*, October 2006, http://www.smithsonianmag.com/history/abraham-lincoln-only-president-have-patent-131184751/.

112. **ALTERNATIVE FACT.** Leonardo da Vinci was a prolific inventor, but scissors were invented roughly three thousand years before he was born.

113. **FACT.** Mario Aguilar, "Charles Darwin Hacked Together His Own Office Chair Because He Was a Genius," *Gizmodo*, July 27, 2012, http://gizmodo.com/5929745/charles-darwin-hacked-together-his-own-office-chair-because-he-was-a-genius.

114. **FACT.** "What is a No. 2 Pencil?" Pencils.com, accessed May 5, 2017. https://pencils.com/what-is-a-no-2-pencil/.

115. **ALTERNATIVE FACT.** Fisher did indeed develop the space pen for NASA, but the investment money did not come from taxpayers. Nor did the Soviets stick with using pencils (which carried the risk of chipping off and sending bits of pencil floating through microgravity). They ordered one hundred space pens of their own. Ciara Curtin, "Fact or Fiction?: NASA Spent Millions to Develop a Pen that Would Write in Space," *Scientific American*, December 20, 2006, https://www.scientificamerican.com/article/fact-or-fiction-nasa-spen/.

116. **FACT.** "Are UFOs real? Famous people who believed," *The Telegraph*, April 22, 2009, http://www.telegraph.co.uk/technology/5201410/Are-UFOs-real-Famous-people-who-believed.html. Thomas O'Toole, "UFO Over Georgia? Jimmy Logged One," *Washington Post,* April 30, 1977, https://www.washingtonpost.com/archive/politics/1977/04/30/ufo-over-georgia-jimmy-logged-one/.

117. **FACT.** Walter A. McDougall, *The Heavens and the Earth: A Political History of the Space Age* (New York: Basic Books, 1985), 134.

118. **ALTERNATIVE FACT.** The Soviet Union never banned microwaves.

119. **ALTERNATIVE FACT.** This enduring myth has no basis in fact: meta-analyses of dozens of studies on the relation between the lunar cycle and individual behavior have found no correlation between the two.

120. **ALTERNATIVE FACT.** No correlation has been found between a full moon and either birth rates or rates of conception.

121. **FACT.** Ethan Siegel, "Why Mercury Isn't The Solar System's Hottest Planet," *Forbes*, June 2, 2016.

122. **FACT.** "China's Wall Less Great in View from Space," National Aeronautics and Space Administration, May 9, 2005, https://www.nasa.gov/vision/space/workinginspace/great_wall.html.

123. **FACT.** "Lightning Really Does Strike More Than Twice," National Aeronautics and Space Administration, January 14, 2003, https://www.nasa.gov/centers/goddard/news/topstory/2003/0107lightning.html.

124. **FACT.** Kathryn Prociv, "Reaching for the sky—Chicago skyscrapers and lighting strikes," *Washington Post*, March 18, 2016, https://www.washingtonpost.com/news/capital-weather-gang/wp/2016/03/17/pic-of-the-week-reaching-for-the-sky-chicago-skyscrapers-and-lightning-strikes/?utm_term=.d8e465ecb7d3.

125. **ALTERNATIVE FACT.** While this is a popular theory, there is little tangible evidence that this is where the symbol originated. Eric Grundhauser, "Why We Think Outhouses All Had Crescent Moons in Their Doors," *Atlas Obscura*, March 28, 2017, http://www.atlasobscura.com/articles/outhouses-crescent-moons.

126. **FACT.** "Film Historian: 'Psycho' Altered Ideas On Censorship," *NPR*, June 18, 2010, http://www.npr.org/templates/story/story.php?storyId=127937275.

127. **ALTERNATIVE FACT.** The first couple depicted on prime time in bed together were the actors (and real-life couple) Johnny and Mary Kay Stearns in *Mary Kay and Johnny*—broadcast all the way back in 1947.

128. **ALTERNATIVE FACT.** Mr. Rogers never served in the military. He went straight from high school to college then began working in television.

129. **ALTERNATIVE FACT.** This popular myth never actually existed, but originated in Michael Crichton's pseudo-historical novel *The Great Train Robbery* and has taken on the appearance of fact. Jeremy Stern, "A Tale Worthy of Poe: The Myth of George Bateson and his Belfry," *History News Network*, October 28, 2013, http://historynewsnetwork.org/article/153726.

130. **FACT.** Simon Usborne, "Eclipsed in Death," *The Independent*, November 22, 2013, http://www.independent.co.uk/voices/comment/eclipsed-in-death-we-remember-jfk-but-what-about-aldous-huxley-or-cs-lewis-8957192.html.

131. **ALTERNATIVE FACT.** The remains were consistent with a man deformed by scoliosis, but without the severe hunchback described by the Bard.

132. **FACT.** Charlotte Endymion Porter, ed., *Shakespeariana*, vol. 1 (Philadelphia: Leonard Scott Publishing Co., 1884), 240.

133. **ALTERNATIVE FACT.** Yes, ninety-six men died during the building of the dam, but all were recovered.

134. **FACT.** Vikas Khatri, *Greatest Wonders of the World* (New Delhi, India: V&S Publishers, 2012).

135. **FACT.** Sewell Chan, "Inside the Brooklyn Bridge, a Whiff of the Cold War," *New York Times*, March 21, 2006, http://www.nytimes.com/2006/03/21/nyregion/inside-the-brooklyn-bridge-a-whiff-of-the-cold-war.html.

136. **FACT.** "Memorial Milestones: Important moments in Arch history," *St. Louis Magazine,* accessed May 7, 2017, https://sites.stlmag.com/arch/.

137. **FACT.** Joanna G. Cantor and Carissa Bluestone, *Fodor's Big Island of Hawaii*, Second Edition (New York: Fodor's Travel, 2009), 87.

138. **ALTERNATIVE FACT.** Though the stats on the Grand Canyon are accurate, it is neither the longest or deepest canyon in the world. That distinction goes to the Yarlung Tsangpo Grand Canyon in Tibet, which is about thirty miles longer than the Grand Canyon and drops a whopping 17,567 feet (28,271.3m)—more than two miles deeper than the southwestern gorge.

139. **FACT.** "Electrical Power Generation at Niagara," NY Falls, accessed May 27, 2017, http://nyfalls.com/niagara-falls/faq5/; "Niagara Power Project," NY Power Authority, accessed May 27, 2017, http://www.nypa.gov/power/generation/niagara-power-project.

140 **FACT.** "Great Pacific Garbage Patch," *National Geographic*, accessed May 27, 2017, http://www.nationalgeographic.org/encyclopedia/great-pacific-garbage-patch/.

141. **FACT.** Rachel Mills, "20 seriously weird places around the world," *Rough Guides*, December 2, 2016, https://www.roughguides.com/gallery/20-seriously-weird-places-around-the-world/.

142. **FACT.** Richard Howells, *The Myth of the Titanic* (London: Palgrave Macmillan, 1999), 141.

143. **FACT.** Alissa Walker, "The Largest Earthquake in U.S. History Happened 50 Years Ago Today," *Gizmodo*, March 27, 2014, http://gizmodo.com/the-largest-earthquake-in-u-s-history-happened-50-year-1552447376. Richard Pallardy, "Chile earthquake of 1960," *Encyclopedia Britannica,* https://www.britannica.com/event/Chile-earthquake-of-1960.

144. **FACT.** Bruce Parker, *The Power of the Sea: Tsunamis, Storm Surges, Rogue Waves, and Our Quest to Predict Disasters* (New York: St. Martin's Press, 2010), 153.

145. **FACT.** Though some maintain that the superstition originated in ancient Egypt, the evidence points to it starting much more recently. Natalie Wolchover, "The Surprising Origins of 9 Common Superstitions," *LiveScience*, September 19, 2011, http://www.livescience.com/33507-origins-of-superstitions.html.

146. **ALTERNATIVE FACT.** Franklin made no mention of tossing salt over one's shoulder, and as best as folklorists can tell, the tradition goes back centuries, originating from the idea that the salt will keep the devil away.

147. **FACT.** Charles Panati, *Extraordinary Origins of Everyday Things* (New York: William Morrow, 1987).

148. **FACT.** Q. Edward Wang, *Chopsticks: A Cultural and Culinary History* (Cambridge, UK: Cambridge University Press, 2015), 11.

149. **FACT.** Margaret Visser, *The Rituals of Dinner* (New York: Penguin Books, 1992).

150. **FACT.** Bethanne Patrick, *An Uncommon History of Common Courtesy: How Manners Shaped the World* (Washington, DC: National Geographic Society, 2011), 102.

151. **FACT.** Margaret Visser, *The Rituals of Dinner* (New York: Penguin Books, 1992).

152. **FACT.** "Super-slippery surfaces: How to empty the ketchup bottle every time," *The Economist*, December 3, 2016, http://www.economist.com/news/science-and-technology/21711015-and-improve-power-plants-too-how-empty-ketchup-bottle-every-time.

153. **FACT.** Andrew Smith, ed., *The Oxford Encyclopedia of Food and Drink in America, Second Edition* (Oxford University Press, 2012), vol. 2, 262–264.

154. **ALTERNATIVE FACT.** The current Oreo design is likely an interpretation of a more explicit floral design that Nabisco created in 1952, with the circle with two bars across the top which contain the word "OREO" is a variant of the Nabisco logo. Nicola Twilley, "Who Invented the Oreo? The Unsung Heroes of Cookie Design," *The Atlantic*, June 13, 2011, https://www.theatlantic.com/entertainment/archive/2011/06/who-invented-the-oreo-the-unsung-heroes-of-cookie-design/240357/.

155. **FACT.** *Inventive Genius (Library of Curious and Unusual Facts)* (Virginia: Time-Life Books, 1991), 73.

156. **ALTERNATIVE FACT.** Despite its reputation, absinthe has never had hallucinogenic properties. German scientists tested old bottles of the "Green Fairy" and found nothing that could cause hallucinations, with the levels of thujone (the active chemical component in wormwood) at the same level as the absinthe that's sold today. Alexis Madrigal, "Sorry, Absinthe Trippers, Scientists Say You're Just Really Drunk," *Wired*, April 29, 2008, https://www.wired.com/2008/04/sorry-absinthe/.

157. **FACT.** Alexandra Ossola, "That Worm at the Bottom of Your Mezcal Isn't a Total Lie," *Motherboard*, October 17, 2014, https://motherboard.vice.com/en_us/article/that-worm-at-the-bottom-of-your-mezcal-isnt-a-lie-1.

158. **FACT.** Deborah Blum, "The Chemist's War," *Slate*, February 19, 2010, http://www.slate.com/articles/health_and_science/medical_examiner/2010/02/the_chemists_war.html.

159. **FACT.** John F. Mariani, *Encyclopedia of American Food and Drink* (New York: Bloomsbury, 2013).

160. **ALTERNATIVE FACT.** There is no such bar, but there *is* an opera house that straddles the border of those same cities: The Haskell Free Library and Opera House.

161. **ALTERNATIVE FACT.** This tag was put in place as a warning to sellers of pillows and furniture (not buyers) not to replace the stuffing of the products with subpar materials (which was a problem decades ago).

162. **FACT.** Mike Orcutt, "Nanocapsules Sober Up Drunken Mice," *MIT Technology Review*, February 17, 2013, https://www.technologyreview.com/s/511261/nanocapsules-sober-up-drunken-mice/.

163. **ALTERNATIVE FACT.** While hangovers are caused by a number of factors, there is scant evidence that drinking more ever helped anyone overcome their symptoms.

164. **ALTERNATIVE FACT.** While one study did find that beer could help with rehydration, the majority of research points to it being a bad post-workout option: it interferes with muscles' rebuilding process. Devon Jackson, "The Truth About the Post-Workout Beer," *Outside*, January 16, 2015, https://www.outsideonline.com/1928696/truth-about-post-workout-beer.

165. **FACT.** Ross Pomeroy, "Sorry! Orange Juice Will Not Cure Your Cold," *Real Clear Science*, December 13, 2011, http://www.realclearscience.com/blog/2011/12/for-the-last-time-orange-juice-will-not-cure-your-cold.html.

166. **FACT.** Aaron E. Carroll, "Sorry, There's Nothing Magical About Breakfast," *New York Times*, May 23, 2016, https://www.nytimes.com/2016/05/24/upshot/sorry-theres-nothing-magical-about-breakfast.html?_r=0.

167. **FACT.** "Ship Shake Cap'n Crunch Liquid," *Mr. Breakfast*, http://www.mrbreakfast.com/cereal_detail.asp?id=318.

168. **ALTERNATIVE FACT.** I made all this up.

169. **ALTERNATIVE FACT.** While this was the public relations version of why the name change came about, it was actually the first word in the name that caused issues. In 1990, the Commonwealth of Kentucky trademarked its name (in part to help it get out of debt), requiring anyone using the name of the state for business purposes to pay licensing fees. KFC's executives decided against doing so.

170. **FACT.** Erin Brodwin, "These Crazy Pictures Show How Companies Use Bugs to Make Red Dye for Food and Cosmetics," *Business Insider*, October 27, 2014, http://www.businessinsider.com/how-farmers-make-red-dye-from-bugs-2014-10/#cochineal-insects-native-to-central-and-south-america-thrive-on-one-particular-species-of-cactus--the-prickly-pear-1.

171. **ALTERNATIVE FACT.** Mascara and many other cosmetics contain guanine, a coloring agent that, despite the similar-sounding name, does not derive from bat dung.

172. **FACT.** Daniella Martin, *Edible: An Adventure Into the World of Eating Insects and the Last Great Hope to Save the Planet* (Boston: New Harvest, 2014), 54–67.

173. **FACT.** Mikaela Conley, "Nutmeg Treated as Drug for Hallucinogenic High," *ABC News*, December 9, 2010, http://abcnews.go.com/Health/large-doses-nutmeg-hallucinogenic-high/story?id=12347815.

174. **ALTERNATIVE FACT.** The two bars were actually released nine years apart. The "3 Musketeers" referred to three smaller, separate bars of different flavors—the form in which the candy originally came.

175. **FACT.** H. Douglass Goff, Richard W. Hartel, *Ice Cream, Seventh Edition* (New York: Springer, 2013), 5. Andrew Smith, ed., *The Oxford Encyclopedia of Food and Drink in America, Second Edition* (Oxford University Press, 2012), vol. 2, 310–311.

176. **FACT.** Paul Collins, "You Say It's Your Birthday," *Slate*, July 21, 2011, http://www.slate.com/articles/arts/culturebox/2011/07/you_say_its_your_birthday.html.

177. **ALTERNATIVE FACT.** Relatives of the composers of the modern version of the song deny it has any connection to the Mass, and early versions of the song going back to the seventeenth century back this up. Although some Scottish politicians and representatives of the Catholic Church did raise concerns about the song as recently as 2008, it was never actually banned.

178. **FACT.** Antonia Fraser, *Marie Antoinette: The Journey* (New York: Anchor, 2002), 135.

179. **FACT.** David Hackett Fischer, *Paul Revere's Ride* (New York; Oxford University Press, 1994), 110.

180. **FACT.** Drew Hansen, "Mahalia Jackson, and King's Improvisation," *New York Times*, August 27, 2013, http://www.nytimes.com/2013/08/28/opinion/mahalia-jackson-and-kings-rhetorical-improvisation.html.

181. **FACT.** Justin Taylor, "5 Myths about Rosa Parks, the woman who had almost a 'biblical quality,'" *The Washington Post*, December 1, 2015, https://www.washingtonpost.com/news/acts-of-faith/wp/2015/12/01/5-myths-about-rosa-parks-the-woman-who-had-almost-a-biblical-quality/?utm_term=.55bf89443f55.

182. **ALTERNATIVE FACT.** Parks was not actually the first black woman to refuse to give up her seat. Nine months before Parks' famous bus ride, Claudette Colvin was arrested on a Montgomery bus for the same violation. Why Parks' proved the watershed moment may have been due to her deeper connections in the local civil rights and Christian community.

183. **FACT.** Columbia University, National Center on Addiction and Substance Abuse, *Women Under the Influence* (Baltimore: The Johns Hopkins University Press, 2006), 21.

184. **FACT.** "Bob haircut celebrates 100th birthday," *Telegraph*, January 9, 2009, http://fashion.telegraph.co.uk/news-features/TMG4206376/Bob-haircut-celebrates-100th-birthday.html.

185. **FACT.** Jess Blumberg, "A Brief History of the Salem Witch Trials," *Smithsonianmag.com,* October 23, 2007, http://www.smithsonianmag.com/history/a-brief-history-of-the-salem-witch-trials-175162489/. "Salem Witch Trials," *History.com*, http://www.history.com/topics/salem-witch-trials.

186. **FACT.** "Scold's Bridle," *BBC: A History of the World,* http://www.bbc.co.uk/ahistoryoftheworld/objects/MUbKwlRsRZ6YP-4QuviCdA.

187. **ALTERNATIVE FACT.** Although there was a "Judas Cradle"—a stool with a wooden pyramid on top of which the punished had to sit—there was no such thing as "Judas Shoes."

188. **ALTERNATIVE FACT.** Neither Puritans nor Pilgrims ever wore buckles on their hats, despite popular images of them doing so. This fad didn't take off until the 1800s.

189. **FACT.** "Concealed shoes," June 19, 2012, https://northampton museums.wordpress.com/2012/06/19/concealed-shoes/.

190. **ALTERNATIVE FACT.** The rule likely originated in the late 1800s as the wealthy sought ways to set themselves apart from the middle and lower classes by inventing arbitrary new fashion rules that only those "in the know" followed.

191. **FACT.** Margo DeMello, *Feet and Footwear: A Cultural Encyclopedia* (Santa Barbara, California: Greenwood Press, 2009), 75, 107.

192. **FACT.** Andrew Adam Newman, "Why Time Stands Still for Watchmakers," *New York Times*, November 27, 2008, http://www.nytimes.com/2008/11/28/business/media/28adco.html.

193. **FACT.** Tanya Cooper, *Searching for Shakespeare* (New Haven, CT: Yale University Press, 2006), 56-57.

194. **ALTERNATIVE FACT.** "Euthanasia Cruises, Ltd." was a hoax perpetuated in 1993 by prankster Alan Abel and has popped back up a few times since.

195. **FACT.** Jeanne Sahadi, "Pennies and nickels cost more to make than they're worth," *CNN Money*, January 11, 2016, http://money.cnn.com/2016/01/11/news/economy/u-s-coins/.

196. **ALTERNATIVE FACT.** The Fed does shred five thousand tons of paper currency a year, but none of the pulp is used in new bills—that would compromise the quality and appearance of the new currency.

197. **ALTERNATIVE FACT.** The term *piggy bank* actually comes from the fact that the pots where people of Western Europe stored their money were made from orange clay known as *pygg*. By the eighteenth century, the term *pygg jar* transitioned to *pig jar* as potters simply cast the banks in the shape of the animal.

198. **ALTERNATIVE FACT.** Some currency does feature a star next to the serial number, but it is a "replacement star" used to indicate a bill that is printed with an identical serial number as another bill.

199. **FACT.** Evan Andrews, "11 Things You May Not Know About Ancient Egypt," *History.com*, November 12, 2012, http://www.history.com/news/history-lists/11-things-you-may-not-know-about-ancient-egypt.

200. **FACT.** John A. Wilson, *The Culture of Ancient Egypt* (Chicago: The University of Chicago Press, 1951), 195.

About the Author

Alex Palmer is the *New York Times* best-selling author of *The Santa Claus Man* and the fun fact books *Weird-o-Pedia* and *Literary Miscellany*. He has written for *Smithsonian*, *Mental Floss*, *Slate*, *Vice*, *Esquire*, and more. Find out more at alexpalmerwrites.com.